M

MW00426234

bureaucratic insanity

Bureaucratic Insanity

The American Bureaucrat's Descent into Madness

S. J. Kerrigan

CLUB
ORLOV
PRESS

Bureaucratic Insanity:
The American Bureaucrat's Descent into Madness

Publication date: April 10, 2016

ISBN-13: 978-1530989522
ISBN-10: 1530989523

Club Orlov Press
http://ClubOrlovPress.blogspot.com
cluborlovpress@gmail.com

"We turn our backs on nature; we are ashamed of beauty. Our wretched tragedies have a smell of the office clinging to them, and the blood that trickles from them is the color of printer's ink."
—Albert Camus

"He has erected a multitude of new offices, and sent hither swarms of officers to harass our people and eat out their substance."
—*The United States Declaration of Independence*

Foreword

When we think of bureaucrats, we imagine officious, unimaginative and generally unremarkable persons. They are depressing to observe, as they repetitiously act in exact accordance with a set of procedures, most of which were created without their input, consent or even their understanding. Under some circumstances they might move you to pity, but interaction with them soon cures you of that impulse. It doesn't matter if you are in a rush. It doesn't matter if you tell them a heartbreaking story of an innocent child in urgent need of help. It doesn't matter if they know you personally. It doesn't even matter if they actually *want* to help you. Through a series of pressures—both economic and psychological—the bureaucrat's allegiance is first and foremost to the written rules. With almost religious refrain, they reply: "I'm sorry, but we regretfully cannot"—at least not until you fill out these forms, attain written permission, or generally climb an ever-rising mountain of paperwork which, they assure you, serves a legitimate and necessary purpose.

Think of the biblical judgment of King Solomon, who initially decided that an infant child be cut in half to satisfy a dispute between two women, both claiming to be its real mother. The threat of such a murderous compromise led one of the women to agree to give up the child to the other rather than see it killed. But the other woman agreed with the decision to kill the child. In this way, Solomon discovered who the real mother was. He then changed his ruling and gave the child to the real mother—who would rather lose her child than see it killed.

In using such a test to get at the truth, Solomon showed that he was wise enough to dispense justice and to rule. But if Solomon were not the king of Israel but a contemporary American bureaucrat, would he have bothered to alter his initial decision? While killing an innocent child would have been pointless, irrational and cruel, decisions like this are not uncommon in a society that values the certainty of absolutist rules over the often imprecise and messy concept of justice.

Where King Solomon was able and willing to act creatively to solve problems, contemporary American bureaucrats are increasingly constrained to taking specific actions as a condition of their continued employment and financial security. Whether you are the head of sales at a company or a modest officer worker, you are expected to adhere to strict rules of conduct, working within hierarchies and obeying strict and detailed rules. These rules are intended to increase efficiency and to guarantee that a product or service has a consistent and predictable quality. Within the contemporary workplace, employees are not free to pursue their tasks however they would like: a condition of their continued employment, they must follow specific instructions that are laid out for them by their superiors. Even the CEOs of major corporations must obey certain conventions, lest they be replaced by someone more conventional. At the edges of corporate officialdom there are brightly colored warning markers they dare not cross, for fear of finding themselves back among the helpless members of the poorer classes.

To one degree or another, we are all subject to such restrictions, and as the number and complexity of rules have increased, so too have the restrictions. No longer are we working and living creatively, finding joy in our inventiveness and the spontaneity of daily life. Instead, we have become like gears in a machine, with all of our actions and relationships predetermined—a nation of automatons, stressed out not just from overwork, but from *inhuman* work that requires precise adherence to standards we may not understand imposed by people we have probably never met.

A bureaucrat functions within an organization, interpreting and acting on its rules. A bureaucrat is not a free agent with complete and total freedom, but someone who, as a condition of employment, submissively serves a higher authority. While this term is broad enough to be applied to many official positions going back thousands of years, the first use of the word was in the early days of the French Revolution, from *bureau*—which is French for 'desk' or 'office.' *Bureaucratie*, when the term was first coined, was seen by some as a new form of government, fundamentally different from previous forms of social control. The term was introduced in 1759 by the economist Vincent de Gournay, who called it "a sickness which is wreaking havoc." Condemning the establishment's use of such organizational methods, the radical newspaper *Le Père Duchesne* called it a "new mode of servitude."[1]

Bureaucracies have always had a reputation for being stolid and unresponsive. When you are interacting with a bureaucracy, you may be talking to another human being, but you are not *dealing* with a human being. Instead, you are deal-

---

1 Bureaucrats and Bourgeois Society: Office Politics and Individual Credit in France 1789-1848

ing with a set of rules and policies. The person you are speaking to has little to no say in how these rules are applied or interpreted. When bureaucracies function well the impersonal nature of the bureaucrat isn't an issue, but when bureaucracies malfunction or target people in an aggressive and hostile way they find themselves at the mercy of an uncaring, dehumanized automaton. For as long as there have been bureaucracies, they have been both appreciated for their efficiency and hated for their impersonal and unsympathetic nature. Ever-ready to increase efficiency, the introduction of ever-more rules and policies is the bureaucrat's standard solution for any discrepancy between an action and its intended outcome.

When a person is deemed to be in violation of a rule, the rule is not reconsidered—to determine whether the proposed punishment is fair in that particular situation, whether the rule is being interpreted correctly or even if the rule has any value to begin with. If you refuse to follow the labyrinth of regulations, you are not considered an individual exercising moral autonomy. Instead, you are branded a rebel. Even if the term is applied generously and with admiration, that it is used at all is intended to demonstrate that written rules are the sole source of legitimacy. The burden falls on the rebel, who must prove that the rule either doesn't or shouldn't apply.

Whether our rules carry the force of law is less significant than we might think. Far too often, the existence of the rule serves as its own justification, regardless of whether it carries with it any moral or legal authority. Within highly regimented societies, the societal norm is that any reconsideration of a rule must originate from the same place within a hierarchy where the rule was created. Those lower in the hierarchy have to go through a series of appeals before they can challenge a rule.

Life doesn't always make sense, and many events cannot be predicted or explained through ideology, our experiences, or the lessons taught to us in school. Viewed objectively—that is, without the crutch of our internal narratives—life appears chaotic and that chaos causes stress. In an advanced industrial society, rules are not stray anomalies that come and go, nor are they optional, but must be followed no matter what chaos reigns or how little sense they make. Our jobs require us to fill out time sheets or document paid time off. Our schools require permission slips for even the most mundane activities. Our political and judicial systems, once prided for their simplicity, are now bloated well beyond the comprehension of even the most knowledgeable lawyers. To understand even a part of how our society functions requires years of schooling and hands-on experience. The practical effect of all this is that much of our life has become incomprehensible to us. And if we don't understand how the world works, how can we hope to find our place within it?

A friend of mine recently recalled an instance in which he conversed at length about America's numerous rules with a foreigner, who found many of them pointless. The young man was sent to the US to learn how to provide customer service for a credit card company (and to eventually replace my friend). He complained that America had so many rules that it was difficult to keep track of them all. He wondered why he had to stop at a stop sign or a red light even if there was no other traffic. Countries with a history of highly regimented industry tend to enshrine rules with a special status that often defies common sense.

There is a tendency in the industrialized world, and in the United States in particular, to adhere precisely to the letter of the law over giving precedence to individual autonomy that requires a more nuanced approach to problematic situations. To many Americans, rules have an almost sacred quality; they are not guidelines or suggestions, but *dictates* that can be reinterpreted only slightly, if at all. Rules, especially written ones, truly do rule. The Ten Commandments define our morality. Our job requirements are defined by an employment contract.

Our crimes and punishments are rarely decided by a jury or a judge who might have a reason to decide based on a concept of justice. Most often, they are decided by a system of plea bargains and minimum sentencing laws which keeps individual human judgment to a minimum. Legal loopholes that provide tax benefits are prized and lobbied for because lawyers know that it is the letter of the law that matters most, not the law's stated purpose.

It is not just the sheer number of rules that is oppressive but their total domination of our personalities. A good setting in which to observe these rules in action is American retail, where public-facing employees are required to provide "outstanding customer service." Of course, this means being attentive to customer anxieties and addressing whatever desires they might have, but it also means putting on a show, being suffocatingly sweet and cheerful to each and every customer they interact with, regardless of whether the customer is in a bad mood or even downright abusive.

Erving Goffman

As sociologist Erving Goffman observed, the purpose of these policies is the "bureaucratization of the spirit" by which employees "can be relied upon to give a perfectly homogeneous performance at every appointed time." Workers must continually suppress their honest emotions, which typically range between indifference and mild disdain, in favor of playing the role of the eager employee who is always happy to help. Their real personalities and feelings are smothered, giving rise to feelings of hostility and aggression that don't go away but are merely masked, both from the public and from the workers themselves, who become alienated from their true selves.

Within bureaucracies, social arrangements are dominated by our assigned roles rather than by our spontaneous and genuine natures. Individuals who would normally be free to engage each other honestly and with sincere emotions are forced to become actors, performing a script which appears caring and kind, but consciously or subconsciously the average worker is resentful because the assigned role is superficial and meaningless.

Within American society, one solution to this pervasive meaninglessness is to pursue a rigid absolutism, a conscious or subconscious insistence that inane rules be followed exactly even when better alternatives do exist. This quest for purity gives some meaning to the meaninglessness. The inane rules with which we are regularly forced to comply are given substance through the committed insistence that they be followed. Since most bureaucrats feel that they cannot effectively challenge the myriad of rules dominating their lives, many of them find meaning by faithfully embodying them. Strict interpretation and execution of these rules becomes their identity and a part of their self-esteem.

Such rigid absolutism can be found throughout American society, but can be observed most readily in education, where new rules on data collection force teachers to judge students solely on their ability to score highly on tests. Students are seen not as human beings who need to be nurtured but as assets or liabilities whose value is based on their performance. Teachers have been turned into data-obsessed bureaucrats, ready to do whatever it takes to make students meet quantifiable standards of performance.

This has been happening for quite some time, but what is relatively new is the displacing effect it has had on our values. Law enforcement personnel, lawyers, teachers and even regular people who don't fit into any of these categories have become preoccupied with harsh punishments designed to put people in their place. Rationalizations such as "I am only doing my job," "We have rules for a reason," and "It's the law" have become common, intended to diffuse criticism and avoid considering the moral ramifications of their actions.

This adherence to uniformity and standardization can be found across American society, but nowhere is the obedience to the written rule more obvious than in America's hierarchical systems of control—our schools, government offices, corporate workplaces, the military and prisons. Within these organizations, individual decision-making is filtered through the chain of command. Individuals who rebel are sanctioned. But what happens when the rules themselves are broken, where the predetermined punishments for breaking certain rules are themselves unjust? Do Americans show the moral courage to defend each other from such bureaucratic absurdities, or do they enthusiastically enforce unjust punishments to comply with bureaucratic dictates? The sad reality is that, for a number of psychological reasons, Americans simply won't stand up for each other—even when the victims are children.

To act with moral autonomy—as a caring human being capable of seeing the nuances in a situation—takes courage, vigilance and a willingness to challenge authority, sometimes at great personal risk. A society that values both psychological comfort and micromanaged control produces few people who display such qualities.

Moreover, some bureaucrats derive a perverse pleasure from inflicting pain on others. The impulse to punish with extreme prejudice erupts out of the hollowness of their collective lives. They engage in vicious acts, punishing the weakest members of our society to satisfy their insecurities. They suspend ten-year-olds for making "finger gun" gestures in school, classifying this as a "level-2 look-alike firearm." They charged a seven-year-old with misdemeanor battery because he threw a piece of candy at his friend's head. They handcuffed an autistic seven-year-old to a chair and charged him with two counts of battery after he attempted to kick a school administrator and a police officer.

These examples, and dozens more described throughout the book are sure to leave you both angry and amused. Despite our protests, there is within these examples a good cause for *Selbstschadenfreude*—taking pleasure in one's own misfortune. There is something compelling about the vulgarity and the cruelty of these excesses.

However, wallowing in bureaucratic inanities is not our objective. *Bureaucratic Insanity* is not a pejorative meant to demean the small-mindedness of bureaucrats, but a diagnosis. Many bureaucrats are so detached from reality that they qualify as clinically insane. They are lunatics who happen to be running the asylum, and who therefore must be either avoided or placated. If we are to keep our own sanity, we must learn to regard them as such.

Having worked for years in a dehumanizing office environment, I know this kind of pressure all too well. A decade ago, fresh out of college, I was grateful to find a secure, relatively well-paying job, but over time a kind of quiet desperation set in as the meaninglessness and the repetitive nature of the work slowly ate away at my self-esteem.

The hyper-controlled workplace, of a sort increasingly common in the US, discouraged honesty. Instead, it preferred to funnel as many decisions as possible up the hierarchy, limiting worker input. The higher-ups distrusted individual initiative. Our products were middling and our services were mostly unhelpful, and sometimes even counterproductive, for our clients. The workplace environment wasn't particularly abusive, but there was simply no reason to ever feel excited about spending 40 hours a week doing something of no importance to anyone. As the economic crisis of 2008 took its toll on the business, the number of inane rules meant to squeeze every last bit of productivity out of the employees became maddening.

Like many working Americans forced to cope with uncaring bureaucracies, I repressed my true feelings for as long as I could, taking comfort in the little prestige I was allotted and in the good pay that allowed some semblance of freedom outside of work. I would take excursions through the park or take long vacations across the country, searching for some kind of elusive, secret peace. But eventually the depression I felt along with my colleagues became harder to ignore. I often lashed out at my friends over minor slights to my ego. I was fortunate enough to have a support network that allowed me to escape that environment before the situation spiraled out of control.

After I decided to leave, I was subtly ridiculed by my former coworkers for being weak. They insisted that I should have been content with having a "good job" and should have concentrated on developing a "good work ethic." At the time, I wasn't entirely sure they were wrong. Looking back, it's clear that my depression wasn't due a lack of vision, but rather the result of lying to myself about my situation. Since then, I have worked hard to find a healthy source of meaning in life. For me, my escape was more than just a physical or an emotional escape from an absurd situation; it was the understanding that life, if lived without meaning, would be ultimately destructive to me and harmful to everyone else in my life that I cared about.

Sadly, many of us are unwilling or unable to extricate ourselves from such situations. Wallowing in denial, we allow official and unofficial rules to control almost every bit of our lives. Life takes on a static, stagnant quality. Without the ability to change life's circumstances, our purpose in it becomes uncertain. If everything is predetermined for us, what is the point of being alive? Why not just go on a sort of autopilot, never making any real decisions and simply playing out our social roles? Many people find reason to do just that: life's material rewards are far more plentiful when we shut up and follow the rules. But robot-like behavior eventually takes its toll. For some, a meaningless life leads to depression while others resort to violence, lashing out in merciless, sadistic bouts of blind, inflexible, dogmatic frenzy.

For many, the solution to our widespread alienation from ourselves is to strike out aggressively. As Marshall McLuhan once observed, "All forms of violence are quests for identity." As our sense of purpose fades, institutional sadism threatens to become the defining characteristic of our time. Ultimately, it isn't racism or classism or any other type of "ism" which perpetuates this simmering hostility, but self-loathing that is the inevitable byproduct of a meaningless existence.

This book is an attempt to understand the times we are living through, to see where our bloated mechanisms of social control have led us and are likely to lead us in the future. We will start by looking at examples of the near-criminal behavior of America's bureaucrats, whose search for consistency causes them to abuse the weak. Their pursuit of robot-like uniformity, combined with the stress of being forced to function in a world that makes no sense, engenders a bitter, venomous hostility that bursts forth in unexpected ways. The first three chapters are devoted to a thorough examination of the phenomenon of bureaucratic violence.

Inevitably, when analyzing such a widespread problem, an investigation of the surrounding culture becomes essential. Why did the United States and other parts of the industrialized world create an army of unthinking, occasionally vicious human automatons? How did the institutions that control our society manage to create such twisted motivations? What is it in our culture that allows us to suspend human decency and promote crass indifference? The out-of-control bureaucracy can't be viewed in a vacuum, as though it alone were responsible for our nation's rampant hostility toward any minor deviation from the norm. In order to understand the origins of institutional sadism, we must explore the history of obedience, and examine the operation of free will within civilizations generally. These questions are answered in detail in the chapters that follow.

We will conclude by addressing what still might be done to reverse our course nationally as well as individually. While bureaucracies are highly resilient to change, there is much we can do to protect ourselves from some of their more aggressive overreaches through self-sufficiency and avoidance. We'll also suggest ways we can insulate ourselves from the psychological pressures of living in an insane society of bureaucrats, and instead build a life worth living.

"We seek alien victims rather than the real source of our rage, since we cannot recognize the truth and are unable to admit our own despair. And the more we express our rage, the more intense it becomes. If we don't discover its cause, our pathological state worsens, and eventually produces a magical image of self and world. We feel invulnerable when we can victimize others, even torture them, without recognizing that it is our own helplessness that is being crushed."
—Arno Gruen

1. Hysterical People

In January 2013 a South Philadelphia fifth-grader went to school with a piece of paper that resembled a gun. It was obviously just a piece of paper and not useful for making a threat, never mind launching a projectile. According to media reports, the girl said her grandfather had made it and that she had forgotten it was in her pocket. It wasn't an elaborate design, simply a sheet of paper with one corner folded over. When she went to school and threw it away, another student noticed the paper looked like a gun and informed the teacher. The girl was suspended and claims she was searched by the school faculty in front of the other students.

In an interview with television reporters, the girl said:

> [A school administrator] yelled at me and said I shouldn't have brought the gun to school. I kept telling him it was a paper gun, but he wouldn't listen.

"I'm waking up at three o'clock in the morning, and my daughter is in the bathroom, crying," her mother said. "She said, 'I'm having nightmares. I'm having dreams that [the school administrator is] chasing me down the street.'"

The girl said that her fellow-classmates were tormenting her. Crying into the camera she said, "They would call me a murderer."[2]

This girl's story—of a harmless action being met with a harsh response from bureaucrats—has become tragically common. That same month, a five-year-old was suspended for ten days for allegedly threatening to shoot another student with a "Hello Kitty Pink Bubble Gun" which she did not have in her possession at the time. The threat was allegedly made at a bus stop before school. The family's attorney said the student was then interrogated by school administrators for three hours without the parents' knowledge. After the parents met with administrators the sentence was reduced to a two-day suspension.

"This logic, which was not said in malice, came from the mind of this beautiful five-year-old child who was playing with her friends, whom she hugs every day," her father said. "This shows how hysterical people who work at schools have become since [the school shooting at] Sandy Hook."[3]

These and other situations like them are a uniquely American phenomenon. They usually stem from a policy called "zero tolerance," a general term usually referring to rules for imposing harsh and mandatory punishments that disregard specific circumstances or mitigating factors. Like mandatory sentencing requirements and "three strikes" laws which are designed to punish serial offenders in the criminal justice system, zero-

2 https://www.nydailynews.com/news/national/grader-hassled-bringing-paper-gun-class-article-1.1245647
3 http://www.huffingtonpost.com/2013/01/18/kindergarten-suspension-pink-bubble-gun_n_2507017.html

tolerance policies take disciplinary discretion away from principals and teachers. While these policies gained prominence in the late 1980s, recent events have prompted even stricter observance, excessively punishing students for even the most minor offenses.

The Sandy Hook Elementary school shooting in December of 2012 took the lives of 26 people, including 20 first-graders. It launched a national debate about gun control, mental health procedures and school safety in general, but (as is often the case in the United States) this concern eventually dissipated without resulting in any meaningful action. But it did cause a fit of gun-related paranoia among school administrators, who are now ready to act against any action or gesture that has even the most tenuous relationship to threats or guns.

Several months after the shooting at Sandy Hook, a seven-year-old Maryland student was suspended for eating a pastry in such a way that it came to resemble the shape of a gun, which school officials claimed he pointed at another student. The boy's father said his son was attempting to shape the square pastry—similar to a Pop-Tart—into the shape of a mountain. School officials at the elementary school say he pointed the pastry at a classmate—though the child maintains he pointed it at the ceiling.

"In my eyes, it's irrelevant," the boy's father said in an interview with the Washington Post. "I don't care who he pointed it at. It was harmless. It was a danish... I feel this is just a direct result of society feeling that guns are evil and guns are bad and if you make your pastry into a gun, you're going to be the next Columbine shooter... Kids are losing time in school for nothing more than playing."

Two years after the incident, school officials claimed the boy's actions were part of a history of class disruption, but the boy's father said he was never made aware of any problems. "I don't think he was suspended because he was being rowdy," he said. "I think he was suspended because of the sensitive nature of the topic."[4] He also wondered whether the pretend-gun offense at age seven would become part of his son's permanent record that would haunt him later in life. "That may sound far-fetched, but, you know what, in today's world, it's possible."

The school sent a letter to the school's parents noting that a "student had made an inappropriate gesture." It also noted that a "school counselor is available to meet with any students" troubled by the incident. It concludes by reminding parents to tell their children "of the importance of making good choices."[5]

On December 21, 2013, a first-grader attending a public school in Montgomery County, Maryland was suspended for making a "finger gun" and saying "pow." The school portrayed the incident as a threat "to shoot a student."

The family's attorney said that the child had no intention of hurting anyone. "He's skinny and meek," he said replying to a media inquiry. "In his words, he was playing." He noted that a record of the incident was likely to create future problems for the child. "They took the worst possible interpretation of this little child's actions, and five years from now, if he gets into a tussle, they're going to look back and say, 'This is one bad little kid.'"

School officials declined to offer specific details about the situation, but they emphasized that the decision to suspend was not taken lightly and was preceded by other incidents.[6]

A few months later, a student in Columbus, Ohio was given a three-day suspension for making a finger gun, classified by the school's officials as a "level 2 look-alike firearm." The boy's

---

4 http://patch.com/maryland/annapolis/boy-suspended-over-poptart-gun-loses-bid-to-clear-school-record
5 http://www.washingtonpost.com/local/education/anne-arundel-second-grader-suspended-for-chewing-his-pastry-into-the-shape-of-a-gun/2013/03/04/44c4bbcc-84c4-11e2-98a3-b3db6b9ac586_story.html
6 http://www.washingtonpost.com/local/education/boy-6-suspended-from-silver-spring-school-for-pointing-finger-like-a-gun/2013/01/02/21acc8d4-54fc-11e2-8b9e-dd8773594efc_story.html

father told the media that according to a letter from school officials his son had pointed it "execution-style" at another child and would be given a longer suspension or permanently expelled if the behavior persisted.[7]

After this situation drew national attention through mocking media reports, Ohio state senators began drafting legislation (S.B. 167) that would eliminate the zero tolerance policy and allow school boards to consider a broad range of factors before electing to suspend or expel a student, "including prevention, intervention, restorative justice, peer mediation, and counseling." To date, neither this bill, nor any like it, has been passed in Ohio.[8]

Zero-tolerance policies are being reviewed in schools across the country in an effort to minimize the more egregious and publicly recognized abuses resulting from blind, judgment-free application of these blunt instruments. But harsh punishments for trivial offenses are part of a society-wide trend, expanding beyond school doors. Inability or unwillingness to address questionable behavior in measured, compassionate ways extends far beyond simple paranoia or vigilance triggered by recent school shootings—which would at least be understandable, if not justified.

Public awareness of the potential for school shootings has clearly increased over the last few decades, especially since the incidents at Columbine High School in 1999 and the more recent shooting at Sandy Hook Elementary. Certainly, some additional vigilance on the part of officials is warranted. However, many school administrators interpret the new, stricter rules in such a way as to deliberately harass students. In some cases, students are clearly justified in their actions, but because they technically violate some poorly worded rule, administrators feel justified in imposing the harshest penalties

---

7 http://www.cnn.com/2014/03/04/us/ohio-boy-suspended-finger-gun/index.html?hpt=hp_c2
8 http://www.acluohio.org/legislation/2013-2014-sb-167

allowed.

This is not to say that gun violence is an illusion. Indeed, mass shootings in the United States are fairly common, but the issue is not gun violence; the issue is that school administrators seem incapable of dealing with complicated situations. They react aggressively, punishing innocent, and sometimes even virtuous children, based on poorly designed policies. Consider Adrionna Harris, a sixth-grader from a Virginia middle school, who in March of 2014 witnessed another student cutting himself with a razor blade. According to media reports, Harris took the razor blade from the student and threw it in the trash. She then comforted the boy until school administrators took over. Most people would consider the girl a hero, but even after Harris had explained the situation school administrators saw it fit to give her a ten-day suspension, with the possibility of expulsion, because she admitted that she was temporarily in possession of a razor blade, and razor blades are prohibited on school property.

"I took the razor blade, and then I threw it away immediately," Harris said during a television interview. "I didn't carry it around the school. I didn't use it against anyone." News reports note that the school agreed that her depiction of the events was accurate.

"I felt she did the right thing," her mother said. "Under the circumstances, she thought he would bleed out, as he was cutting himself, and there was no teacher in sight. It was a 911 situation, and there wasn't time to find a teacher."

Any clear-thinking person can see that the girl's actions were justified—even heroic—but school administrators wanted to punish her based on her very transitory and unavoidable handling of a razor blade. Any reasonable person would conclude that there is something seriously wrong with them. Indeed, the school administrators proved deaf to the voice of reason. But they did react to public embarrassment: it was only after the media became involved that the girl's hearing was moved up and the punishments originally handed out were nullified.[9]

In November of 2013 a Tennessee man was arrested and charged with disorderly conduct after objecting to a school policy which forbid children from walking home. The policy was ostensibly instituted to prevent students from walking home alone. While other parents chose to drive their children home, he wanted to walk home with them. The school refused to release his children to him and the School Resource Officer (a police officer stationed at the school) arrested him. In a six-minute video recorded by his fiancée, which later went viral on the internet, the man can be seen conversing with the officer. At no point during the recorded exchange does the man raise his voice or act threateningly. In a media interview, the officer said that while he agreed that the policy was wrong in principle, he still had to do his job "enforcing the law."[10]

It seems outlandish to think that the officer in question is lacking all common sense or judgment; something else must be wrong with him. Plainly, what he did was a willful, vicious, violent act. It would be wrong to see this and other similar abuses as mere side-effects of schools becoming generally more draconian and controlling. More accurately, they reflect a complete unwillingness to show mercy or to be flexible when considering the circumstances of a situation. Such essentially psychotic behavior on the part of those entrusted with the care of children can be neither explained away nor excused; we must examine it and find ways to address its root causes.

Even students who honestly attempt to follow the rules can be punished for purely technical transgressions. Just before the end of the 2013 to 2014 school year, a Pittsburgh-area elementary school suspended first-grader Darin Simak for acci-

9 http://wavy.com/2014/03/19/student-suspended-for-taking-razor-from-self-harming-classmate/
10 http://www.theblaze.com/stories/2013/11/19/school-is-out-my-kids-are-to-be-given-to-me-dad-arrested-after-objecting-when-school-says-he-must-wait-to-take-his-children-home/

dentally bringing a toy gun to school. His mother claims she had packed his school bag for him, but had failed to notice the toy. When about an hour before the end of the day Darin realized that the toy was in his possession, he reported it to his teacher, who then sent him to the principal's office and gave him a suspension. When interviewed by news media, his father asked, "What was he supposed to do? Just hide it and keep it in his bag so he doesn't get in trouble? He did the right thing, and we're trying to teach him the right way and now they're teaching him the wrong way."[11]

Students do not need to be even theoretically capable of actually causing any harm in order for the punishment to be severe. Food, pieces of paper, plastic toys, and even imaginary objects can be construed as evidence of malicious intent that must be severely punished. In February of 2015 a fourth-grade student from a West Texas school pretended to have the magical "one ring" featured in JRR Tolkien's books *The Lord of the Rings* and *The Hobbit*, in which it has the power to turn the wearer invisible. The school suspended the nine-year-old after he said that he had the ability to make his friend disappear. His father said in an email, "I assure you my son lacks the magical powers necessary to threaten his friend's existence. If he did, I'm sure he'd bring him right back." This wasn't the first time the boy had problems in school: in the six months since they moved there he had been suspended twice before, including in-school suspensions for calling a black classmate black and for bringing to school his favorite book: *The Big Book of Knowledge*, which contains a picture of a pregnant woman.[12]

---

11 http://news.yahoo.com/blogs/oddnews/first-grader-suspended-and-facing-expulsion-after-finding-toy-gun-in-backpack-and-even-turning-himself-in-203058288.html

12 https://www.polygon.com/2015/2/1/7960307/fourth-grader-suspended-lord-of-the-rings;

http://www.nydailynews.com/news/national/texas-boy-suspended-bringing-ring-power-school-article-1.2099103

Another instance of innocuous behavior punished severely occurred in New York City in 2010, where a junior high school student was handcuffed, arrested and held for seven hours at a police station for writing on her desk at school. According to a report by the Associated Press, a Department of Education spokesperson admitted that this incident was a mistake, but then the student still had to do eight hours of community service and write a book report on what she had learned.[13]

In 2011, a Florida seventh-grader was arrested and charged with misdemeanor battery after throwing a Tootsie Pop at his friend's head. According to the boy's attorney, the boy who was hit and his father had to go to court and state under oath: "We don't want to press charges for this, it was a piece of candy." Only then did the state attorneys drop the charge, but the arrest for battery will continue to appear on his record. The charge was made under the school district's zero-tolerance policy.

If you think that such incidents are a rarity, you would be mistaken. In 2005, in Florida alone there were more than 28,000 school arrests. That number dropped to 13,780 in 2012, but students can still be arrested for any kind of disorderly conduct, such as talking back to a teacher or any behavior that seems disrespectful.[14]

Arrests for bad behavior such as throwing food are not limited to Florida. A report by the ACLU noted that Mississippi had numerous instances where such harmless behavior had been referred to law enforcement. In at least one case, five students were charged with felony assault for throwing peanuts. The report's summary noted:

In 2000, what began with a few students playfully throwing peanuts at one another on a school bus ended

---

13 http://www.huffingtonpost.com/2010/02/05/desk-doodling-arrest-alex_n_450859.html
14 https://stateimpact.npr.org/florida/maps/map-florida-students-arrested-for-bad-behavior-not-criminal-behavior/

in five Black male high school students being arrested for felony assault, which carries a maximum penalty of five years in prison. When one of the peanuts accidentally hit the white female bus driver, the bus driver immediately pulled over to call the police, who diverted the bus to the courthouse where the students were questioned. The sheriff commented to one newspaper, "[T]his time it was peanuts, but if we don't get a handle on it, the next time it could be bodies."

This statement boggles the mind: is the sheriff in question that stupid, that vicious, or both? And is he psychologically healthy enough to be allowed to serve in an official capacity?

The same ACLU report highlights a half-dozen other instances where equally disturbed reactions from school officials and police resulted in the arrest of children. In one case, a five-year-old was held in the back of a police car for "violating the dress code." According to the report, his mother said that "her son's school required solid black shoes, and despite her best efforts to cover them with a black marker, red and white symbols were still visible on his black shoes. When she followed up with her son's principal, he justified his actions by telling her that her son needed to be 'taught a lesson.'" [15]

School officials have even opted to discipline students for perceived slights against authority that merely mimic serious offenses. The Roanoke Times reports that a Virginia sixth-grader was recently suspended for an entire year after school officials found a leaf in his backpack that they suspected was marijuana. Prosecutors were forced to drop the possession charges after three separate drug tests confirmed that the leaf was not marijuana. However, the boy was still forced to attend an alternative school for problem students. There he is searched for drugs twice a day and is evaluated for drug abuse problems. His parents say the school's reaction has taken a toll on their son. The boy, previously normal and happy, is now

15 http://b.3cdn.net/advancement/bd691fe41faa4ff809_u9m6bfb3v.pdf

seeing a psychiatrist for depression and panic attacks.[16]

In an op-ed, the Washington Post warned that "imitation" drugs are grounds for discipline: "It doesn't matter if your son or daughter brings a real pot leaf to school, or if he brings something that looks like a pot leaf—okra, tomato, maple, buckeye, etc. If your kid calls it marijuana as a joke, or if another kid thinks it might be marijuana, that's grounds for expulsion."[17]

In April of 2015 a 14-year-old Florida boy was charged with a felony for accessing his teacher's computer and changing the image of the desktop background "to annoy him." According to a news report, the student discovered the computer's administrator password by looking over his teacher's shoulder while he was typing it in. It was easy to guess what was being typed in because the password was simply the teacher's last name. Police insist that the felony charge was warranted because the computer contained sensitive testing data related to Florida's Comprehensive Assessment Test or FCAT, even though the test results were encrypted. School officials felt justified in involving the police because a ten-day suspension, which he also received, was not deemed sufficient.

Though they admit that the student did not attempt to access or alter grades, Sheriff Chris Nocco said: "Even though some might say this is just a teenage prank, who knows what this teenager might have done." Apparently, the mere potential to commit a crime, even if it was imaginary, given that the test results are encrypted, was itself considered a crime. Nocco continued, noting that the real purpose of the felony charge was to send a message to other students: "If information comes back to us and we get evidence [that other kids have

16 http://www.roanoke.com/news/columns_and_blogs/columns/dan_cas ey/casey-not-pot-gets-th-grader-in-big-trouble/article_67dc2868-0f0a-53c0-96ad-595a88391aa3.html

17 https://www.washingtonpost.com/news/wonkblog/wp/2015/03/16/vir ginia-school-suspends-an-11-year-old-for-one-year-over-a-leaf-that-wasnt-marijuana/

done it], they're going to face the same consequences."[18]

The unstated but clear belief is that punishments must be a fable for public consumption, to terrorize others into compliance. Justice and rehabilitation are beside the point. To quote the philosopher and historian Michel Foucault: "The ceremony of punishment, then, is an exercise of 'terror.'... If severe penalties are required, it is because their example must be deeply inscribed in the hearts of men."[19]

While the written rules gave school administrators and the police adequate discretion to impose punishment that was appropriate to the situation, their reaction at all levels was to abuse the rules to maximize the damage to this child's future. Only a charge of terrorism could have been more absurd, but given the level of malice being demonstrated regularly by those in positions of power, even this is to be expected at some point.

Such disproportionately severe punishments are not confined to America's schools. In recent years, the judicial system has begun to dole out punishments that are cruel and unusual —something that is unconstitutional under the Eighth Amendment. In Utah, thirteen-year-old Kaytlen Lopan was convicted for cutting the hair of a toddler against the parent's wishes, who pressed assault charges. District Juvenile Judge Scott Johansen sentenced Kaytlen 30 days in a juvenile detention center. He also told the mother that Kaytlen could avoid an additional 150 hours of detention if she agreed to cut off her daughter's hair in retaliation. Reluctantly, the mother agreed, cutting her daughter's hair "off clear up to the rubber band" as instructed by the judge.

"She definitely needed to be punished for what had happened," her mother later told local news. "But I never dreamed it would be that much of a punishment." The mother admits

---

18 http://www.tampabay.com/news/publicsafety/crime/middle-school-student-charged-with-cyber-crime-in-holiday/2224827
19 Michel Foucault, *Discipline and Punish*, p. 49

that she may have made a mistake by agreeing to the eccentric ruling, "I guess I should have went into the courtroom knowing my rights because I felt very intimidated. An eye for an eye, that's not how you teach kids right from wrong."[20]

In another instance, Painesville Municipal Court Judge Michael Cicconetti told Diamond Gaston, who was charged with assault, that she could serve 30 days in jail or submit to being pepper-sprayed by her victim. She agreed to be pepper sprayed. The judge then switched the pepper spray with harmless saline spray without telling Gaston. According to news reports, Cicconetti said he wanted her to feel pain, but not physical pain.[21]

Jonathan Turley, who teaches law at George Washington University, has been consistently critical of judges who attempt to be creative in the courtroom, charging that their real motivations are personal, not judicial:

> These sentences make justice a form of public entertainment and allow judges to turn their courtrooms into their own macabre productions. While judges talk a good game about their effort to be creative, they clearly enjoy this role and the publicity that comes from making people demean themselves. It appeals to the lowest common denominator of our society and unfortunately there are many who enjoy [seeing] others degraded. Indeed, some appear to be working through their own serious issues or yielding to their own emotional impulses in [imposing] punishments...[22]

20 http://www.news.com.au/world/eye-for-an-eye-judge-gives-utah-mum-option-to-chop-off-daughters-ponytail/story-e6frfkyi-1226407014692
21 http://cleveland.cbslocal.com/2015/05/29/judge-courtroom-pepper-spray/
22 http://jonathanturley.org/2015/06/01/welcome-to-painesville-ohio-judge-orders-woman-to-either-accept-jail-or-being-sprayed-in-eyes-with-pepper-spray/#more-90605

Even the homeless, who have few assets, can find themselves targeted by overzealous rule enforcers who are incapable or unwilling to make an exception to the rules. Consider James Brady, a homeless resident of northern New Jersey, who found $850 in an envelope on the sidewalk. Brady acted nobly and reported his discovery to police, saying later that he didn't want to take money from someone who was worse off than he was. After waiting six months for the owner to step forward, Brady was awarded the money.

However the bureaucracy wasn't through with him. When Brady went to apply for general assistance and Medicaid benefits, it was denied to him for the rest of the year because he had failed to report the money he had found as income! The director of human services told the newspaper they were just following the rules.

"I'm sorry but we had to—I had to—follow regulations," she said. "He only pays five dollars [a month] in rent."

"This is stupid," Brady said. "I had already proven my honesty by turning in the $850. They were treating me like I was a dishonest individual, like I was trying to cheat them out of the money."

A few years earlier, Brady was a photographer and a market analyst, but Brady claims that he was traumatized and couldn't work after nearly dying at the World Trade Center on 9/11. Now, without Medicaid, Brady will be unable to continue his therapy or receive treatment for any of his other health problems.[23]

In December of 2014, three students in Rochester, NY were arrested while waiting for a school bus. Their basketball team was gathering there because it wasn't a school day, when a police officer arrested them. According to the police report, the three were arrested for "Blocking pedestrian traffic while standing on a public sidewalk" and "preventing free passage of

---

23 http://www.northjersey.com/news/hackensack-samaritan-loses-benefits-over-850-he-found-and-turned-in-1.626086

citizens walking by and attempting to enter and exit a store."

One of the boys said, "We tried to tell them that we were waiting for the bus. We weren't catching a city bus, we were catching a yellow bus. He didn't care. He arrested us anyways."

When their basketball coach showed up and tried to mediate the situation, he was threatened with arrest as well. He said, "One of the police officers actually told me, if he had a big enough caravan, he would take all of us downtown."

A few days later, the district attorney said in a public statement that "in interest of justice" the charges would be dropped.[24]

In May of 2015 a school superintendent pressed charges against four attendees of a Mississippi High School graduation ceremony after they had begun cheering and calling out the names of some of the graduates. They were charged with disturbing the peace and police issued a warrant for their arrest. A video of the incident shows some of the attendees cheering (but not excessively) in support of the graduating class. They admit that they knew they might be asked to leave if they made noise during certain parts of the ceremony, but were surprised when they were served with a court notification.

"It's crazy," one of them said. "The fact that I might have to bond out of jail, pay court costs, or a $500 fine for expressing my love, it's ridiculous, man. It's ridiculous."

Local news reported that the superintendent felt that pressing charges was warranted. He said he was determined to have order at the ceremonies and insisted "negative attention" would not be tolerated.

"I can understand they can escort me out of the graduation," one of the women said, "but to say they are going to put me in jail for it? What else are they allowed to do?"[25]

---

24 http://www.msnbc.com/politicsnation/were-teens-arrested-bus-stop-profiled
25 http://fox40.com/2015/06/03/warrants-issued-for-people-who-cheered-at-high-school-graduation/

Albuquerque, New Mexico may be the most aggressive city in America in the way it handles minor offenses. In the years 2006 to 2011, Albuquerque police shot 38 people, more than half of whom were mentally ill. In a population of 550,000, the rate of fatal shootings by police is eight times that of New York City.[26] Authorities there recently mulled a decision to try an eight-year-old as an adult.[27] Police handcuffed a seven-year-old autistic boy to a chair after he attempted to kick school administrators and a police officer. They later charged the child with two counts of battery.[28] The Department of Justice later published a report describing the culture in Albuquerque as one "that emphasizes force and complete submission over safety."

District Attorney Kari Brandenburg said there was a good deal of public support behind the police within the city. When approached by people in public about the more violent actions of police, they would say things like, "I think the police are doing a good job, and they ought to shoot more criminals."

"[They're] not evil people," Brandenburg said defending the city's heartless residents. "But they lack understanding. They talk as if it doesn't matter if somebody were to die."[29]

Individually, the reactions of school administrators, police officers and other rule enforcers could be explained away as an unfortunate oversight, a misunderstanding, or simply just poor reporting on the part of news networks who sometimes only get to hear one side of a story. Having worked in the press for years, I recognize that this last criticism is especially hard to dispel, since news reporters often do fail to get both sides of a story. This is further complicated by the unwillingness of school administrators to comment on specific student inci-

26 http://www.newyorker.com/magazine/2015/02/02/son-deceased
27 http://www.tucsonnewsnow.com/story/9320428/8-year-old-charged-with-two-counts-of-first-degree-murder
28 http://www.abqjournal.com/72509/news/parents-of-autistic-boy-file-suit.html
29 http://www.newyorker.com/magazine/2015/02/02/son-deceased

dents while parents are almost always ready to convey the full level of their disgust.

Nevertheless, all of the above, taken as a whole and combined with my plentiful personal experiences, makes it clear to me that there is a willingness on the part of many bureaucrats and mid-level administrators to act aggressively, without regard to individual circumstances and without compassion. Even when they are given an opportunity to use discretion for the benefit of the community, bureaucrats in America show that they have a greater allegiance to absolute uniformity and written rules than to the community they are supposed to serve. The glut of stories involving harsh punishments relating to children indicates that something is amiss. Nor is this a passing phase: the frequency of these incidents is increasing.

I submit that as our society has become more regimented, micromanaged and generally "rule-ridden," we have seen a corresponding increase in absolutist and acompassionate thinking on the part of officials. Internal pressures within organizations such as schools, corporations, and government agencies have only exacerbated these tendencies.

In examining the growth of bureaucratic rules and regulations within America's school systems and other bureaucracies, we will first consider the organizational systems themselves: the schools, the corporations, government agencies and all the other authority structures that often demand such inhuman behavior. What is it about these social systems that removes the moral sensitivity of teachers and school administrators—people who are supposed to look out for the weakest and most vulnerable members of society? We will also see how these systems allow such heartless and ultimately irrational rules to be written. Moreover, just because poorly constructed rules exist, this doesn't mean that they must be followed; we will need to assess the psychological conditions that result in such merciless practices.

Finally, we will examine American culture itself. How can a society which prides itself on being hyper-competitive and individualistic simultaneously strive to dismantle individual autonomy so completely? By looking at other cultures, we will see how regimented, industrialized societies excel in dismantling communal human interaction in favor of predictable, robot-like behavior.

Such complaints and observations have been documented many times by authors writing from many perspectives. The willingness of individuals to obey authority figures and written rules has been steadily documented ever since the dawn of sociology and psychology. Political struggles within governments often use pressure to encourage others to obey the dictates of a central authority. Since the earliest civilizations, the military has developed methods for ensuring unquestioning loyalty and prompt obedience. During the industrial revolution, financial tools and economic pressures were used to compel individuals to perform repetitive and precise actions. To better serve the machines that were being developed at that time, there was a need to not only control human action, but to regiment it in accordance with very precise time restrictions. Over time, even our thoughts and emotions have come to be micromanaged through a decidedly robotic system of control required for "professionalism." All of these trends are linked, and all of them signal a deterioration in compassionate behavior. What will come next, and where will it end, as the human race is subjected to an ever-increasing level of automation, while control and efficiency continue to be the guiding principles of an increasingly totalitarian bureaucracy?

Many of these questions have already been answered, or at least addressed, by others. But only recently has obedience to bureaucratic dictates reached such extreme levels of perversion at all levels of society. The implementation of new policies like zero tolerance has transformed school officials and other bureaucrats into unthinking automatons.

The frequency of horrendous acts perpetrated for the sake of rules and authority is continuing to increase. These stories would border on comical, if only they weren't so perverse. There's a venomous streak of wrath hidden behind a façade of detached, unemotional law and objective policies. Obedience, conformity, rationality, and absolute consistency are replacing love of spontaneity, freedom, diversity, and exuberance.

If human decision-making has already been so curtailed by overzealous and robot-like authority figures, what will happen to tomorrow's victims when the pressure increases even further, forcing people to obey even more commands from a central authority, overruling their own better judgment? What good is it to be human if you cannot make decisions for yourself? What kind of community is filled with spiteful bureaucrats intent on making life so unpleasant and difficult?

Imagine a world where all decisions are made by a centralized authority, where school officials, police and other rule-enforcers have no choice but follow whatever the central planners dictate. This is not science fiction; the technologies of adaptive artificial intelligence and ubiquitous surveillance make it possible to micromanage every action and to automate even punishment. This assessment is needed now, because the next step could well be either a sudden reversal—a return to a more human way of living—or, if conditions continue to deteriorate, an erasure of all remaining intellectual and moral freedom. There is every reason to believe that in the future restrictive controls on individual behavior will dramatically increase. While bureaucrats may not engender much sympathy, their hostile actions must be understood. Rampant, arbitrary, increasingly automated bureaucracy is a potentially terminal cultural disease. We ignore it at our peril.

"And always, everywhere, there would be the yelling or quietly authoritative hypnotists; and in the train of the ruling suggestion givers, always everywhere, the tribes of buffoons and hucksters, the professional liars, the purveyors of entertaining irrelevances. Conditioned from the cradle, unceasingly distracted, mesmerized systematically, their uniformed victims would go on obediently marching and countermarching, go on, always and everywhere, killing and dying with the perfect docility of trained poodles."
—Aldous Huxley

2. The zero-tolerance society

Zero-tolerance policies first began making an appearance in America's schools in the early 1990s. In 1994, President Clinton signed a law requiring the states to adopt rules to expel students who brought weapons to school. This law expanded upon another law passed four years earlier that created stiff penalties for people who knowingly carried weapons into school zones. The US Constitution allows states to overturn or ignore federal laws, but doing so would have led to loss of federal funding. Since then, these prohibitions have been widened to include items that could be used as weapons, drugs, alcohol, types of clothing which might indicate gang membership and more.

According to the Department of Justice, during the 2009-10 school year, out of the nation's 32,300 schools, roughly four in ten have taken "serious disciplinary action" against a student, such as expulsion or transfer to a specialized school. In addition, nearly all public schools nationwide have taken some steps to promote student "safety and security." Almost all schools now require a visitor to sign in or check in with school officials and 92 percent now lock doors during school hours. A failure to observe these policies can sometimes come with punishments similar to those imposed on students who bring weapons or drugs to school. In one recent case reported by the local CBS News affiliate, a mother was arrested by St. Louis Police after she attempted to reach her son, who has Asperger's syndrome, after receiving a "frantic" phone call from a teacher who said the boy was "panicking."[30]

The state of Texas has begun fining minors for skipping school at a rate of up to $500 a day. In a typically bureaucratic fashion, students cannot be sent to jail for failing to attend school; rather, they are sent to jail for failing to pay the fines. Students can receive a $300 credit toward their bill by spending a day in jail with adult prisoners. According to a report by Texas Appleseed, a truancy reform nonprofit group, the majority of students who have gone to jail in this way in the last three years are poor. Hispanic, black, and special education students are also overrepresented in truancy cases across the state. Over 1,000 students have been sent to jail for truancy-related offenses over the last three years, including solitary confinement,[31] because minors are not exempt from it. According to one report, "One student was housed in solitary confinement for most of his eleven-day sentence in 2013, being allowed out only to spend 48 hours under suicide watch in the infirmary, according to jail officials."

In a circular bureaucratic nightmare that is typical of juvenile sentencing, students who spend time in jail need to provide proof to the school of their imprisonment or face addi-

30 http://www.huffingtonpost.com/2014/03/21/walnut-groves-mom-arrested-sign-in_n_5009132.html
31 https://www.documentcloud.org/documents/2019199-texas-appleseed-class-not-court.html#document/p12/a214752

tional truancy fines. Students with five or more unexcused absences in a semester can be expelled even after serving time in prison to pay off a truancy-related debt.[32]

"A little stay in the jail for one night is not a death sentence," one judge told a TV news station after he jailed an honors student who had been working multiple jobs.[33]

Shackling juvenile offenders with handcuffs, leg irons, and belly chains is a common practice, even though the vast majority of juvenile offenders are suspected of committing only nonviolent offenses. In one instance, a nine-year-old was shackled for stealing a pack of chewing gum.[34]

In 2005, the Supreme Court ruled that except in extreme circumstances, even those charged with capital murder cannot appear in court while shackled because this would violate their right to due process: if a jury sees them shackled, this can be a cause for declaring a mistrial. Amazingly, this ruling does not apply to minors, who usually see a judge rather than a jury.

Robert May directed "Kids for Cash," a documentary about a judicial scandal in Pennsylvania, where a judge was receiving payoffs for sending juveniles to prison, and was subsequently sent to prison himself. In a Washington Post editorial May wrote:

> It boggles the mind that these protections are not extended to children, but no case involving a shackled juvenile... has reached the Supreme Court. Our crew heard about eleven-year-olds being separated from their families, about kids living in cockroach-infested cells, and about how those experiences led children into a spiral of depression and substance abuse. Still, it was recalling the shackling that made many break down on

32 http://www.buzzfeed.com/kendalltaggart/texas-sends-poor-teens-to-adult-jail-for-skipping-school#.xbLE1Vqob

33 http://www.cbs46.com/story/18626605/texas-honors-student-jailed-for-excessive-truancy

34 http://m.cdapress.com/news/local_news/article_3fca8362-b60d-568a-8dbf-ff9dc4575f20.html?mode=jqm

camera, parents and children alike. For most, it marked the beginning of their journey through a cruel justice system that left the children far more aggressive than before. The shackles sent a message of fear, that the system did not recognize them as children—or human beings for that matter.[35]

Security and student monitoring have been steadily increasing over the last two decades. Commonsense, low-cost measures were adapted first, with more draconian methods of control being introduced every year, including random dog sniffs to check for drugs (in 20 percent of schools), metal detector checks (5 percent), and drug tests for student athletes (6 percent). The courts have been instrumental in transforming schools in the United States into macabre social science experiments. For instance, in a 6-3 ruling the Supreme Court said in 2002 that in part because of the use of locker rooms and because "communal undress is inherent in athletic participation," students have less of an expectation of privacy and therefore could be randomly drug tested. Using this decision as precedent, later that same year the court allowed random drug testing for participants in all school extra-curricular activities, including those that do not involve "communal undress."

School administrators and their defenders in the media may protest, but decisions being made by schools are often unrelated to violence. The penalties sometimes cause serious psychological damage. In 2003, an Arizona middle school strip-searched a thirteen-year-old student under the mistaken belief that she was in possession of an over-the-counter drug— ibuprofen. Bringing in over-the-counter drugs without school permission is against the rules. The student's mother sued, arguing that the search violated the Fourth Amendment to the

---

35 http://www.washingtonpost.com/posteverything/wp/2015/05/08/why
-do-we-still-put-kids-in-shackles-when-they-go-to-trial/?
wpisrc=nl_headlines&wpmm=1

Constitution which protects against unreasonable searches. The case eventually made its way to the Supreme Court, where in an 8 to 1 decision the justices agreed that the strip search was illegal, but since there was no "clearly established law," the school administrators and nurses were protected from liability. The only dissenting opinion came from Justice Clarence Thomas: "Redding would not have been the first person to conceal pills in her undergarments. Nor will she be the last after today's decision, which announces the safest place to secrete contraband in school."

The Supreme Court only muddied the waters by failing to define exactly under what circumstances schools could strip-search students. In January of 2015, a classroom of elementary school students was partially strip-searched so that administrators could check for feces. According to a report by USA Today, the school claimed that an unknown student was defecating in the gymnasium. To find the culprit, they asked about two dozen students to drop their pants, girls in one room, boys in another. The superintendent insisted that the students were told only to lower their pants "just a little."[36]

The increase in such aggressive, acompassionate behavior is not limited to schools, indicating that the reasoning behind zero tolerance is broader than just a change in school culture. For example, the Supreme Court's willingness to allow administrators to strip-search students to eliminate any possibility of drug use parallels their willingness to allow strip searches of anyone suspected of any arrestable offense.

In the 2011 ruling, Florence v. Burlington County, the Supreme Court ruled in a five-to-four decision that the court is not in a position to second-guess local police because, in the words of Justice Kennedy, "People detained for minor offenses can turn out to be the most devious and dangerous criminals." In that case, the victim, Albert Florence, was arrested for failing to appear at a hearing for a fine. He was taken to jail where

---

36 https://www.youtube.com/watch?v=j_qoWH1l6jw

he was strip-searched, then moved to another jail where he was strip-searched again. Eventually the police realized Florence had already paid the fine and released him.

The Fourth Amendment to the Constitution protects people from "unreasonable searches and seizures"; however, the Supreme Court considers it reasonable for a man to be strip-searched for failing to pay a traffic ticket. Thus, you may rest assured that every police department in the United States can strip-search you at any time, for any reason. In an attempt to eliminate any ambiguity, the ideology of zero tolerance has rendered this constitutional protection null and void.

A strip search is an extremely invasive procedure. According to the prison manual used as evidence during the Supreme Court's deliberations, a strip search requires:

> ...a visual inspection of the inmate's naked body. This should include the inmate opening his mouth and moving his tongue up and down and from side to side, removing any dentures, running his hands through his hair, allowing his ears to be visually examined, lifting his arms to expose his arm pits, lifting his feet to examine the sole, spreading and/or lifting his testicles to expose the area behind them and bending over and/or spreading the cheeks of his buttocks to expose his anus. For females, the procedures are similar except females must in addition, squat to expose the vagina.[37]

Strip-search procedures for schools vary by state. Some states forbid the practice. Others allow it provided no school official touches the student.

* * *

Schools in America have expended a tremendous amount of effort in controlling students instead of teaching them.

---

37 Supreme Court case Florence v. Burlington County

Dr. Craig Haney of the University of California, Santa Cruz specializes in the study of institutional environments and the psychological effects of incarceration. In a 2001 paper titled "The Psychological Impact of Incarceration," Haney writes:

> When most people first enter prison, of course, they find that being forced to adapt to an often harsh and rigid institutional routine, deprived of privacy and liberty, and subjected to a diminished, stigmatized status and extremely sparse material conditions is stressful, unpleasant, and difficult.[38]

The description is not dissimilar to the experience of most public school students. Students are made to feel less like they are participants in their own education and more like machines that must produce the particular kind of output that teachers and administrators demand. If they don't comply, they are punished. School bureaucracies have adopted the use non-physical violence and psychological pressure as the primary methods to force students to conform. Like America's prison system, which has also abolished corporal punishment, psychological violence have become the standard method of control. The school system's preference for hiding an appalling level of psychological violence behind a façade of artificial harmony is disturbingly analogous to the worsening situation in America's prisons over the last 30 years.

While outlawing corporal punishment is an improvement, it can be argued that the now standard psychological forms of punishment have more serious and lasting effects. Which is worse—temporary physical pain or lasting psychological anguish? There can be no comparison between a student who is hit on the hands two or three times with a ruler and a student who is arrested and threatened with having to register as a sex offender for running nude across a field at a football game, as was the case at a Maryland High School in 2013. A week later,

---

38 http://aspe.hhs.gov/hsp/prison2home02/haney.htm#II

that student committed suicide, prompting critics to speculate that the school's harsh response contributed to the student's death.[39]

Proponents of zero-tolerance policies have been unable to prove that harsh measures deter infractions, but there is some evidence to suggest that the opposite is true. Treating children as though they are criminals, or including them in populations of seriously troubled students or adult prisoners, only increases the kinds of social delinquency that the authorities claim they are trying to combat. If everyone is a criminal, then no one is, and jail becomes just another adolescent rite of passage. The figures bear this out: according to a study conducted by *Pediatrics*, a peer reviewed journal of the American Academy of Pediatrics, up to 41 percent of Americans are arrested at least once by the time they turn 23.[40] In turn, the criminalization of what is normally considered juvenile but largely harmless behavior is changing the public perception of what it means to be a criminal: to be criminal is merely to be human.

As if this were not enough, an additional problem with zero tolerance is that nobody quite knows what it means. Dr. Brian Schoonover, a school administrator for the St. John's County school district in Florida, writes that a major problem for schools across the country is that different schools choose different interpretations of "zero tolerance":

> School districts often use the same words in their Student Codes of Conduct but associate different meanings to the words. For example, what one district considers a weapon or drug may not be what another district would punish a student for possessing, even if both had policies against the possession of weapons or drugs. One district may apply the term loosely, stating they have a

39 http://nypost.com/2013/10/11/teen-who-faced-sex-offenders-list-for-streaking-commits-suicide/
40 http://pediatrics.aappublications.org/content/early/2011/12/14/peds.2010-3710.abstract

zero tolerance against violence in their district, but never defining for the reader what exactly that means. Other districts may list specific offenses as 'Zero Tolerance Offenses,' but fail to provide specific consequences for those offenses. Still other districts may list specific offenses that result in suspension or expulsion, but choose not to categorize them as 'Zero Tolerance Offenses.'[41]

Unable or unwilling to adhere to broad principles which depend on inefficient and imprecise human judgment, school administrators have continually piled on more clarifications, reinterpretations and entire new rules, keeping individual interpretation of rules to a minimum while demanding perfect obedience. If the rules aren't written just right, students become victims of circumstance.

There is no evidence at all that zero-tolerance policies are effective in deterring violence. This is hardly a surprise: children have little ability to interpret and follow arbitrary and abstrusely worded rules. In addition, far too often the problem isn't with the written policies themselves, which sometimes let the disciplinarians consider mitigating circumstances. Rather, the problem is that the bureaucrats are unwilling to see students as people. In many cases they appear to be intent on following the rules to such a literal degree that their motivation seems to be less about school safety and more about their compulsion to maintain absolute consistency in following the rules. Students are increasingly treated as objects to be manipulated to achieve abstract managerial goals.

The purpose of zero-tolerance policies is to reduce violence and criminal behavior in schools. But the effect of zero-tolerance policies is to dole out psychologically damaging punishments. That this is sometimes done with apparent glee by trigger-happy school administrators and teachers is itself a form of violence which, given the amount of psychological damage

41 Brian Schoonover, *Zero Tolerance Discipline Policies*, p. 50-51

it causes, should be considered criminal. In all of the examples we have looked at thus far, the common characteristic among bureaucrats has been their apparent zeal in enforcing total submission to their precious little rules. Throughout, the common theme is the extreme dehumanization, both of American bureaucrats and their victims. To understand its root cause, the question we must answer is this: What is the psychological process that induces everyday, salt-of-the-earth Americans, as soon as they find themselves in positions of authority, to start using rules and laws to viciously bully and harass the weakest and the most vulnerable?

"I think it's quite possible that the 1960s represented the last burst of the human being before he was extinguished. And that this is the beginning of the rest of the future now, and that from now on there'll simply be all these robots walking around, feeling nothing, thinking nothing."

—From the film *My Dinner with Andre* (1981)

3. The Broader Problem

America's political class has been busy transforming schools into prisons, but neither of these can function without an obedient and indifferent workforce. Slavish adherence to written rules and the unwillingness of authority figures to show any sympathy or understanding toward those in their care extends far beyond school grounds. It is an epidemic that to one degree or another affects all of us. Our society has become impersonal and hostile. We can see the tendency for harsh retribution everywhere: police officers hand out large fines or charge suspects with serious criminal offenses for activities that may have once been considered mundane or juvenile. The police state now recognizes few limits to its power. As horrendous as this power grab has been, it does not explain the increasing willingness exhibited by the low- and mid-level bureaucrats to brandish their rule-books in wanton disregard for basic decency.

While in numerous bizarre cases we can only guess at the motivations of authority figures, we can observe a number of common themes. In most instances where they display rigid adherence to the rules, the following characteristics are clustered together:

1. Robotic and shallow thought patterns; a tendency toward absolutism

In many of these cases, the rule-breaker is technically in violation of some official policy created by other authority figures somewhere else in the bureaucracy. Usually, that part of the equation is not in dispute. The core problem is that rule enforcers are often unwilling to consider pertinent details relating to the specific situation, such as the offender's age, intentions, state of mind, prior record or vulnerable nature. Enforcing the letter of the law, rather than achieving a positive outcome, is the primary goal. The prescribed punishments are draconian while the actions barely justify a verbal scolding or any response at all.

2. Unemotional professionalism interrupted by unseemly bouts of self-righteousness

Many rule enforcers are quick to avoid displaying any emotional response at all—even one that basic human decency might demand under the circumstances. They actively resist appeals to understanding or calls to act empathetically. Occasionally, however, the façade of professionalism will give way to a gleeful eagerness to inflict pain and cause damage. As rule enforcers impose harsh penalties, one can often observe a self-righteous attitude: they are happy to "smack down," "put someone in their place," or "force the square peg in the round hole." Like an abusive parent who punishes a child mercilessly, the rule enforcer claims that the punishments are for the child's own good, lest the child become spoiled.

3. Unquestioning obedience to authority—both to written rules and to a hierarchy

In many of the examples in this book, someone—usually a teacher or a police officer—made a decision to involve a higher authority. There was a willingness, to escalate, advancing the issue higher up the chain of command, and a corresponding unwillingness to take individual responsibility and to act autonomously. Apparently, these people are happy to be "cogs in the machine" and actively avoid making their own decisions. They are always happy to relegate moral responsibility to others. The more hypocritical among them might lament, "If it were up to me, I would rather not." However, their protest rings hollow; they have weighed the situation and have chosen to play it safe in the game of bureaucracy rather than stick out their necks by following their own principles.

4. Infractions seen as existential threats to the all-important order

Finally, infractions, especially ones pertaining to current events discussed in the media, such as school violence, are regarded as existential threats, even though such concern is rarely justified. In schools, the connection between mundane rule-breaking activity and the truly criminal acts—such as school shootings—is tenuous bordering on untraceable, yet even minor infractions are treated with a grave seriousness.

A teacher who observes a student engaging in innocent play—say, by holding a pastry that may, to an overactive imagination, resemble a gun, or wielding a disposable plastic knife in mock combat—must know on some level that this does not pose a threat to public order. Further, knowing the school's embrace of zero-tolerance policies, the teacher must also suspect that the student would not be treated fairly if this incident were escalated. And yet, despite these reservations, many teachers do escalate it by reporting it to school administrators. Through their internal deliberations, they must have determined that there is nothing wrong with the child and that there is no danger to anyone else, yet they choose to enforce rules which they themselves may consider unjust.

A teacher I know described to me one such situation when she was working at a private school. At one point, it had come to the attention of the administration that students were using what they deemed was an excessive amount of bad language. They couldn't agree on what constituted bad language or what punishment would be appropriate for each offense.

"Most of the other teachers were more offended by the students' use of 'Jesus Christ' than anything else," she explained. "I wouldn't even consider that worthy of a punishment at all." The eventual consensus was that there would be a "clampdown" on all bad language, including words like "crap" and even "crud." A kind woman, she often expressed a sincere desire to help children work around the rules, but admitted that when the pressure was on, she would enforce them. "I was walking by a student's desk just as he dropped a folder on the floor and he said 'crap.'" she said. "I thought to myself, 'Really Johnny? You had to say that right as I was walking by in front of all these other kids? Now you have to get detention and you will lose your recess time.'"

Just recently, I had a friend confide to me that his work had instituted a "point system" policy for calling out sick, because "apparently employees cannot be trusted to tell the truth." To avoid accumulating points, he would need to notify them the day before. In one such instance, he notified them at 3 a.m. for his shift set to begin in about six or seven hours, only to be told later that he was being given points for failing to notify them early enough. He asked the company's head of human resources if he had done anything wrong and she admitted he did not, but insisted that she had to assign him points, saying, "It's company policy." "I asked her if she could simply look the other way," my friend said to me. "There is no oversight. It's not like she would be risking her job. She admitted I did nothing wrong, but just faithfully executed the policy as it was written."

Whenever I ask friends or colleagues why they think these admittedly unsympathetic decisions are being made, they are quick to point to financial considerations, both at the individual level and for the institutions. Clearly, there are incentives that motivate people to act in harsh, uncaring ways. However, since most of them are not directly financially incentivized to find as many rule infractions as they can, it is reasonable to assume that it is not personal financial gain that motivates them. Instead, there must be some other, psychological force at work.

Is it fear that drives them to submit so eagerly to the bureaucratic machine? Is it fear of losing their job, their healthcare or the respect of their peers? Perhaps they are afraid of being held responsible in the event of an unlikely disaster? There must be some truth to that, because bureaucratic rules do exist, in part, to minimize institutional liability while protecting individuals from the consequences of their own mistakes. However, I doubt that this adequately explains the desire of many bureaucrats to insist on absolute conformity to the rules. What possible harm is there in showing mercy toward a child who accidentally brings a toy gun to school and confesses his mistake? In many instances, the rule enforcer is not under constant surveillance; discretion is possible, but it is often foregone in favor of doling out brutal punishments.

Some education experts have argued that zero-tolerance policies give schools an underhanded way to artificially raise their all-important standardized test scores by labeling low-performing students as troublesome and expelling them. Schoonover, who is an advocate for school discipline reform, notes that "a school's actual grade-letter may increase if enough low performers are removed... some would wonder if the reason [zero-tolerance policies] are so prevalent is so principals have easy ways to [expel] low-performing students from their schools."[42] Schoonover's theory sounds credible, but it doesn't explain the harsh punishments and control methods that don't result in outright expulsion. Moreover, the general climate of fear and hostility created by zero-tolerance rules is unlikely to produce higher test scores.

If it is fear that motivates teachers to lavish psychological abuse on innocent children, this fear may not even be entirely conscious. It might not have anything to do with the threat of losing one's material or social status, but may instead be an irrational fear of autonomous action. Of course, it can also be the path of least resistance: in an already stressful environment, it is less harrowing to follow pre-written scripts for responding to specific situations than to weigh every rule, law and custom on a situation-by-situation basis, all the while looking over your shoulder. Is it an unconscious fear of change, or a fear of the unknown, or a naturally slothful disposition that drives rule enforcers to accept preexisting dictates? Coupled with self-doubt, feelings of inadequacy, and other sources of stress, many authority figures may force bureaucratic prescriptions upon others without even realizing they are doing so in their own selfish self-interest.

While I do not wish to dismiss these explanations outright, they fail to account for instances where the rule enforcers self-righteously embrace harsh punishments even though they are empowered to make autonomous decisions. Why do people willingly, without clear coercion, choose to act in such an aggressive and hostile manner?

Teachers, administrators, and other members of bureaucratic hierarchies are influenced by cultural traits unique to regimented, industrial societies. This includes the constant pressure to be productive. In the United States, there is an unspoken, though widely accepted, belief that without the ability to be productive a person is at best useless and at worst a parasite. But bureaucrats are not directly productive, and so their

---

42 Brian Schoonover, *Zero Tolerance Discipline Policies*, p. 30

sense of self-worth within the organization has to be determined solely based on their ability to conform to the rules. Traits that cannot be quantified—like compassion, patience, and a willingness to see complex situations clearly—are not quantifiable, and therefore not valued.

The bureaucratic environment is oppressive. Beginning in the 1950s the number of American white-collar workers began outnumbering blue-collar factory jobs. Most of us now spend about a quarter of our lives behind a desk of some kind, tasked with processing digital documents. Over time, this can become soul-killing work, but it comes with an aura of high social standing. We feel lucky to have a job that is less physically demanding, that includes the perks of the lackadaisical office life, with ample trips to the coffee machine, the snack vending machine, the water cooler and, of course, the bathroom. Even the humble office desk becomes a symbol of prestige—not to mention the office chair.

But it comes with a cost: gone are the feelings of brotherly solidarity that made tolerable the unionized factory life, where union-men actually called each other "brothers." In comparison to the din and bustle of the factory floor, the office environment is isolating and antisocial—a stale, hypercontrolled environment. The air temperature is regulated, and there are few distractions and little noise. There is no weather, no seasons. Cubicles isolate employees' visual and auditory senses. An environment without distractions promotes productivity, but sensory deprivation also heightens a worker's sensitivity to any stimulus. Observe how office workers will flock to the windows to see a heavy downpour during a summer storm. Office romances are often more volatile than they otherwise would be. Without a way to release tension, people who would normally show patience, tolerance and understanding become short-tempered, agitated and neurotic. At the same time, they are constantly encouraged to suppress their all-too-human urges in the name of professionalism. Suppressed feelings and desires invariably manifest themselves in other ways, of which brief outbursts of aggression are the most obvious.

According to a poll conducted by Gallup in 1955, 44 percent of all workers said they enjoyed their working hours more than their time spent at home. Back then the office was more human: even the lowly office minions could indulge in ribald humor and a bit of backslapping, smoked right at their desks and kept a liquor bottle in the bottom right-hand drawer. Sure enough, a similar poll conducted in 1999 showed only 16 percent of all workers preferred their working hours to home. Political scientist Robert Putnam writes in his book *Bowling Alone*, which chronicles the collapse of American civic community, that "as many as one in four workers is chronically angry on the job and many researchers believe that incivility and aggression in the workplace are on the rise."[43]

While many white-collar workers take a utilitarian and practical approach to their jobs, just seeing it as a paycheck and nothing more, their jobs still have a way of imposing their values upon them. Many Americans are not merely working for a wage; they are working to accomplish their employer's goals. They link their self-esteem with the success of the corporation. In turn, workers who identify with the success of their employer are more willing to engage in exploitative and harmful behaviors in the name of the organization. They are also be much more likely to achieve career advancement and a greater degree of social legitimacy, because internalizing their employer's value system allows them to fit in better.

To be efficient, a bureaucratic system's many moving parts need to act in unison, and since these moving parts are humans, their individuality must be suppressed. The ability to make decisions based on moral concerns often acts as a check on a system's more egregious abuses, making it less efficient. There is usually a direct trade-off between organizational efficiency and human decency. But when bureaucrats, in pursuit

---

43 Robert Putnam, *Bowling Alone*, p. 91

of maximum efficiency, abuse their own colleagues, the colleagues sometimes become violent. More extreme forms of workplace violence include mass shootings, which have also been on the rise over the last few decades, beginning first in small-town post offices, and later metastasizing to offices and schools around the country. Writer Mark Ames documents this quite thoroughly in his book *Going Postal:* "Today these massacres can appear anywhere at any time... with all of the geographic randomness yet circumstantial similarity of a roving guerrilla war." Ames notes that "while the attacker is often labeled whatever the most evil term of the day is (Nazi, racist, Jacobin), that motive doesn't hold up under further investigation, and instead it often turns out the attacker was abused at work... [T]he real enemy isn't the criminal, but the culture that made him snap."[44]

Most abused bureaucrats do not strike out in such a theatrical fashion, instead finding more socially acceptable ways to vent their wrath. The aggressive bureaucrat, forced to remain subservient to the hierarchy above him, experiences a constant drumbeat of low-level shame. Unable to extradite himself from the trap, he lives within it, demanding that others become equally subservient, and making them obey the rules that subjugate him. He commits what Albert Camus called "nihilistic murder" of himself and others.

When discussing bureaucracy generally, the term "crazy" is often thrown around, and I would argue that this characterization is accurate. We must consider that these widespread outbursts and acts of aggression are linked to a mass delusion, a culturally, socially and technologically induced psychosis. People are losing their grip on a part of their humanity. This causes them to act aggressively or to oppress others to a point where they act violently in return.

The more complex a system becomes, the more susceptible it is to a systemic breakdown. Clearly, our work environments

---

44 Mark Ames, *Going Postal,* p. 143, 147

have become very complex, as the number of rules, laws and other controls on our lives has increased. When creating a complex process to control people, the breakdowns result from what in corporate jargon might be described as a "human resource failure." Workplace injuries, resulting in disability claims, are an obvious example. Less recognized, but still common, is the sudden lapse of good judgment, chronic suppression of emotion, or constant dissatisfaction with life resulting in depression or hostility. These aren't the failings of individuals, but of the system in which they find themselves trapped. As a result, we often find ourselves at the mercy of overzealous rule-enforcers who act as if they are our masters.

The relationship between a master and a slave creates silent hostility that cannot be penetrated until the slave is freed. There is no human interaction possible between a master and a slave because their relationship is always overshadowed by the inequality of their relative status. The same is often true of the relationships among the slaves, if they are in competition for status, or if they are trying to become masters themselves—by insisting on observing the rules. Within the contemporary American workplace, this master-slave dynamic is dominant and nearly inescapable. Nowhere is this more apparent than in the school system, where dozens of students are subjected to a single teacher's will. If that teacher has been bureaucratized and has surrendered her sense of sympathy and compassion, the results will likely be disastrous for the students. They become co-opted into the hierarchy as obedient servants, or, if they rebel or are unable to comply adequately, they are labeled defective and discarded.

In 1832, US Congressman James H. Gholson said: "Our slave population is not only a happy one, but it is a contented, peaceful, and harmless one." At the time, this line of reasoning was widely accepted in large part because slave rebellions in the United States were rare. While this view may have seemed obvious to some in the ruling class, it was ultimately a shallow observation that failed to recognize the complexities of slave psychology. The submissive attitude of most slaves was achieved through repeated use of violence, and the promise of more violence against them if they resisted. In some cases, slaves felt responsible to their masters, identifying with their goals and believing that their position was inferior. The now well understood spiritual deprivation that accompanied slavery in America was only rarely interrupted by explicit slave revolts.

Kenneth Stampp, a professor of history at the UC Berkeley, described in his book *The Peculiar Institution* several methods of psychological manipulation necessary to guarantee the compliance of a slave:

1. The slave must be placed upon a footing of "unconditional submission... The slave must know that his master is to govern absolutely and he is to obey implicitly."

2. The slave must feel a sense of personal inferiority.

3. Make the slaves "stand in fear" of the master's power and in his propensity for violence.

4. Get the slave to "take an interest in the master's enterprise and to accept his standards of good conduct." In general, the slave should equate the goals of his master with his own.

5. Create in the slave "a habit of perfect dependence upon their masters."

Of these methods of control, number four is particularly relevant for the bureaucratic mindset. In order for bureaucrats to unquestioningly follow a precise and often inhumane set of instructions, it is enormously helpful if they believe in the broader corporate or governmental goal. But all of these methods can be observed in a contemporary work environment. As economic pressures continue to rise, the worker-employer relationship continues to worsen.

If I could add one additional item to Stampp's list, I would note that the modern slave-master often tries to limit the level of discourse, by making certain subjects taboo and by isolating his slaves from each other, ensuring corrosive ideas do not gain traction among them.

Every day in the US, millions of people get up, shower, get dressed and drive to work. They eat at particular times of the day, lest they miss the opportunity. They follow their boss's instructions, which are sometimes in direct violation of their personal moral code. They pay taxes, even if the money goes toward causes they find morally objectionable. Rebellious people who attempt to escape these restrictions by starting their own business, or by joining the swelling ranks of the unemployed, face hardships and hurdles which make these paths less than desirable.

The requirement that they must conform to the rules is made clear to them early in life. Contrary to the abiding myth that childhood is a happy, free, idyllic time, young people are subject to constant supervision. Work is valued over play. What children want to do is immaterial. Their parents—who are normally the most important individuals in their lives—only see them for an hour or two a day and sometimes on weekends. They take on the role of bossy taskmasters. Over time, children quickly learn to take orders from anyone who acts like an authority figure. For those who naturally resist being bossed around by strangers, the cost of resisting is often harsh. It's expected of them that they learn to accept the path of least resistance, believing in lies, both large and small, that enable them to do so without experiencing major psychological discomfort.

Naturally, when they grow up, they imagine that they really want to get up to go to work, to follow the instructions of authority figures, and to prove themselves within predefined social contexts over which they have no control. Those who adapt well are able conform, appear normal, and indeed be normal—or what passes for normal in a society that demands conformity. The most serious and committed conformists appear to enjoy and find comfort in their ability to fit in, happily avoiding the moral complexities that often come with the exercise of free will.

Early in Aldous Huxley's seminal 1931 novel, *Brave New World*, he argues that in order for a future society to be functional, it would need to make people love their servitude:

> Later on their minds would be made to endorse the judgment of their bodies. "We condition them to thrive on heat... Our colleagues upstairs will teach them to love it. And that... that is the secret of happiness and virtue—liking what you've got to do. All conditioning aims at that: making people like their inescapable social destiny."

Psychologist B. F. Skinner essentially agreed, arguing that "it should be possible to design a world in which behavior likely to be punished seldom or never occurs. We try to design such a world for those who cannot solve the problem of punishment for themselves, such as babies, retardates, or psychotics, and if it could be done for everyone, much time and energy would be saved." Here, he lays out the modus operandi

B. F. Skinner

of all civilization: to control behavior not only for the benefit of production, but for the benefit of its unhappy citizens for their own good.

In *Discipline & Punish: The Birth of the Prison* Michel Foucault writes that properly shaping public attitudes is directly linked to "representation," or how aware the general citizen is of the possibility of punishment. A "gentle way of punishment" can be achieved through a consistent, natural and mechanical nudging toward a certain way of being. "Like the gravitation of bodies," Foucault writes, "a secret force compels us ever towards our wellbeing... Let the idea of torture and execution be ever present in the heart of the weak man and dominate the feeling that drives him to crime." Through constant, largely invisible pressure, these "gentle ways" of positive or negative reinforcement can be employed to achieve any desired social behavior. Only the illusion of autonomy remains.

If obedience is automatic, punishment becomes unnecessary. Skinner's critics would later charge him with attempting to "mechanize" humanity into predictable and controllable outcomes, not for its own benefit, but for the benefit of a central authority. The method of control that has found the most success is to infantilize the masses, then to provide punishments and rewards to keep them passive and obedient. Of course, this is all quite arrogant; such rigid control may be possible when dealing with mechanical devices, but in the domain of human psychology unintended consequences are the norm, not the exception. In the end, the social engineers inevitably turn out to be sorcerer's apprentices, setting in motion processes they can neither understand nor control.

"I do know that for the sympathy of one living being, I would make peace with all. I have love in me the likes of which you can scarcely imagine and rage the likes of which you would not believe. If I cannot satisfy the one, I will indulge the other."

— From the 1994 film, *Mary Shelley's Frankenstein*

4. Robopath Society

In February of 1966 Time Magazine published an article called "The Future: Looking Toward A.D. 2000." The author described a plethora of imaginative predictions about the future, including underwater farms, a fully automated society run by robots where only ten percent of the population is employed and planes that can carry up to a thousand people, which by the end of the millennium "will of course be old hat." These were the usual optimistic predictions you'd expect to read in a periodical from that time, but the "experts" this author went further than most. In a RAND Corporation study, "82 scientists agreed that a permanent lunar base will have been established long before 2000 A.D. and that men will have flown past Venus and landed on Mars." Of course, the article also predicts flying cars and the casual use of mood control drugs to help avoid having to deal with "a wife or husband [that] seems to be unusually grouchy"—a prediction that seems to have been lifted from the pages of Aldous Huxley's *Brave New World* with its happiness-inducing drug Soma.

The Time article went on:

Futurists are earnestly considering all kinds of worries: the possible failure of underdeveloped countries to catch up with the dazzling future, the threat of war, the prospect of super-government. Today's 'New Left' predicts the need for political movements to break up big organization. But the skeptics are plainly in the minority. Some futurists, like Buckminster Fuller, believe that amid general plenty, politics will simply fade away. Others predict that an increasingly homogenized world culture—it has been called "the culture bomb"—will increase international amity...

Harvard's Emmanuel Mesthene, executive director of a ten-year, $5 million program on Technology and Society commissioned by IBM, believes that for the first time since the golden age of Greece, Western man "has regained his nerve" and has come to believe, rightly, that he can accomplish anything. "My hunch," says Mesthene, "is that man may have finally expiated his original sin, and might now aspire to bliss."

In the 1960s, the United States was at the absolute peak of its political, economic and propagandistic power. In less than four years after this article was published, that same nation put a man on the moon. Optimism ran wild. There was a feeling abroad that Americans could achieve anything and solve any problem.

Russian-American sociologist Pitirim Sorokin wrote in his 1941 book *The Crisis of Our Age* that mankind's successes seemed "limitless." His view was that there was a good chance that our culture's embrace of material goods was cyclical and would eventually give way to "ideational" ways of living that focused on ideas, spiritual growth and a broader fulfillment of human needs. Sorkin argued that we were very near the point when humans would make this transition, since there were already so many positive signs. He wrote:

[W]e are proud of man. It is not strange that our culture has become homocentric, humanitarian, and humanistic par excellence. Man is its glorious center. It makes him the measure of all things. It exalts him as the hero and the greatest value, not by virtue of his creation by God in God's own image, but in his own right, by virtue of man's own marvelous achievements.

Pitirim Sorokin

It substitutes the religion of humanity for the religions of superhuman deities. It professes a firm belief in the possibility of limitless progress based on man's ability to control his own destiny, to eradicate all social and cultural evils, and to create an even better and finer world, free from war and bloody strife, from crime, poverty, insanity, stupidity, and vulgarity. In all these respects we live, indeed, in an era of a truly great glorification of man and his culture.

Most writers and futurists of the mid-20th century were of the opinion that the new millennium would bring about the possibility of a society of near endless leisure, productivity, and spiritual growth. Others thought it would be one dominated by totalitarian governments like the one featured in George Orwell's 1984. But a few social thinkers speculated that technology itself might transform human beings on a more fundamental level—indeed, that it might already be transforming people by making our thought processes more machinelike.

Looking at the behavior of America's numerous contemporary rule followers and rule enforcers, it's difficult not to liken them to the numerous preprogramed machines that are now so firmly embedded in our lives. What does it mean to think like a machine? Of course, machines do not think. They act only according to their design, and it is a key, highly desirable feature that they are not able to act independently of that design. In a machine, unpredictable behavior is always classified as a malfunction, or a "bug"—something to be worked around until it can be fixed.

Yevgeny Zamyatin

Consider computer programs. They can examine information they are given, determine if it meets certain criteria, and transform it. But when presented with a new situation, unforeseen by the programmers, they cannot spontaneously decide to reprogram themselves in order to be able to handle it. Much like the bureaucrats we've been describing so far, computers act in accordance with their stated function. However, unlike the bureaucrats, they are far less likely to malfunction (once all the bugs have been fixed) because they need not suppress their personal feelings or desires—they have none—and are therefore not prone to irrational bouts of self-righteousness or hostility.

Computers, and machines generally, systematically follow commands in the exact way in which they have been configured to follow them. They cannot arbitrarily decide to disobey. With simple mechanical devices, the laws of physics are clearly

60

visible: the simplest of these machines operate in ways that are predictable even to the untrained eye. If you use them incorrectly, they cease to function and can even harm you. More complex machines exhibit more complex behaviors which, to the untrained eye, may seem magical, but ultimately their actions are confined by a set of explicit rules.

A computer cannot yet think like a person, but a person can indeed think like a computer. A person acts like a computer by performing actions mechanically—not weighing the morality of their decisions, not considering the unintended consequences of their actions, never acting autonomously in defiance of the rules. Rather than let themselves be guided by their critical faculties, nuanced feelings and intuitions, the human robot mechanically follows a predetermined set of rules.

Dystopian science fiction writer Yevgeny Zamyatin was an early supporter of the Russian Revolution, some of which he witnessed, but became disillusioned as it resorted to increasingly dehumanizing levels of control, coupled with the introduction of industrial mass production, which was just beginning to reshape society at the time. In his novel, *We*, Zamyatin imagines a highly controlled society with structures made of glass—glass being efficient and allowing the government to easily monitor its citizens. People have no names; instead, they are assigned numbers like prisoners. They wear identical clothes and walk in step. Drugs, alcohol and other vices are strictly prohibited. All rights, including reproductive rights, are highly regimented. Even walking partners are assigned. Straight lines, mathematics, time management and absolute submission to authority are the defining traits of this society. Its most important cultural works echo these values with titles like *Mathematical Norms, Flowers of Court Sentences, Those Who Come Late to Work!* and "the popular book, *Stanzas on Sex Hygiene!*" The government's propaganda sings the praises of this society, specifically its sterile formalism and perfectionism.

Our whole life in all its complexity and beauty is thus stamped forever in the gold of words. Our poets do not soar any longer in the unknown; they have descended to earth and they march with us, keeping step to the accompaniment of our austere and mechanical March of the musical State Tower. Their lyre is the morning rubbing sound of the electric toothbrushes, and the threatening crack of the electric sparks coming from the Machine of the Well-Doer, and the magnificent echo of the Hymn of the United State, and the intimate ringing of the crystalline, shining washbasins, and the stimulating rustle of the falling curtains, and the joyous voices of the newest cookbooks, and the almost imperceptible whisper of the street membranes.

Our gods are here, below. They are with us in the Bureau, in the kitchen, in the shops, in the restrooms. The gods have become like us, ergo we have become like gods. And we shall come to you, my unknown readers on another planet, we shall come to you to make your life as godlike, as rational, and as correct as our own.

Zamyatin's *We* depicts a society of strict controls, the result of which is an unemotional and ultra-rational social system. Love, compassion, and autonomy are not only not needed, but are actively avoided by most, because they are a danger to the perfect uniformity of the system.

The protagonist, a man by the name (number, that is) of D-503, is largely stripped of his humanity, and his internal decision-making processes are predictable and obedient. Only after interacting with "criminals" does he discover emotions, dreams, and starts acting out in an uncontrolled manner. Early on, he still longs for the simplicity of purpose offered by the state, for a controlled, mechanical, unambiguous life:

I continue to believe that I shall recover, that I may recover. I slept very well. No dreams or any other symptoms of disease... Everything will again be simple, regular, and limited like a circle. I am not afraid of this word 'limited.' The work of the highest faculty of man, judgment is always directed toward the constant limiting of the infinite, toward the breaking up of the infinite into comfortably digestible portions...

As D-503 attempts to communicate his discomfort in being forced to feel, he says, "In the name of the Well-Doer, please forgive me. I am very sick; I don't sleep; I do not know what is the matter with me." His friend replies, "Yes, yes, I understand, I understand. I am familiar with all this—theoretically, of course."

Zamyatin believed that it was conceivable that society, in an attempt to produce products in an efficient manner, would attempt to strip its inhabitants of their autonomy and their ability to make informed, independent decisions. A society valuing only efficiency would have no need for feelings or art. Instead, there would be mathematics and written absolutes. Such a society doesn't really need people; rather, it needs machines in human form. Since an efficient machine requires precision, any individuals attempting to act on their own personal beliefs or conscience would pose a danger. Could a person actually come to internalize and enjoy these values of mechanistic efficiency and precision? Absolutely. Would such a person then react harshly when exposed to the alien values of autonomy and free will? Very likely.

In many ways, contemporary American society is similarly regimented. But whereas the citizens of Zamyatin's OneState were at least able to comprehend the value of their society's absolute dictates, we are compelled to obey rules that are often incomprehensible, contradictory, or even blatantly self-defeating. As we are driven farther and farther in our national quest for unreasoning obedience, a profound sense of meaninglessness comes to pervade most of our life's actions.

What autonomy still exists is concentrated at the very top. In Zamyatin's dystopia, the pronoun "we" is reserved for the central planners—because they speak for everyone and control everyone. In our world, the use of "we" often disguises an attempt at imposing political uniformity or a triumphalist narrative: that "we"—the great nation, or, worse yet, humanity as a whole—are advancing, not only technologically but socially and politically. This is an assumption that Zamyatin clearly doubts. In the hands of an individual, "we" can mean anything, but in the hands of a technocrat this humble personal pronoun encapsulates within it an entire ideology.

Be it a government bureaucracy, a corporation or even a contemporary nuclear family unit with its prenuptial agreement and individual bank accounts, the more regimented an institution, the more regimented the individuals within it must be. And the more we, as individuals, are forced to interact with corporations, government agencies and schools, the more robotlike our own actions become.

The term *robot* comes from the Czech word *robota*, which means "forced labor, compulsory service, drudgery." The term was first used in the 1920 science fiction play *R.U.R.*, short for *Rossum's Universal Robots*. In what became one of the author's biggest successes, Karel Čapek describes a factory run by robots who look like people, but without souls. With stunning insight, Čapek writes that the promise of robots is that they will one day produce "so much wheat, so much cloth, so much everything that things will no longer have any value." The robots eventually become convinced of their superiority, con-

Karel Čapek

64

demning all that is human to death, even as they continue aimlessly working to produce products.

> Robots of the world, you are ordered to exterminate the human race. Do not spare the men. Do not spare the women. Preserve only the factories, railroads, machines, mines, and raw materials. Destroy everything else. Then return to work. Work must not cease.

Earlier, the play hints at the possibility that the destruction of the human race could have been avoided if the robots were treated with love and allowed to have a soul, but as Commercial Director Busman notes, "That would raise production costs." By keeping labor cheap and dehumanized, profits can rise, lowering prices and providing for the material needs of consumers. As for the owners of the factory, the shareholders, "their only dream was their dividend," Čapek writes. "And it's because of their concern for their profits that mankind is about to perish."

Are Čapek's robots all that different from today's bureaucratic rule enforcers? The robots were committed to their jobs, even to the detriment of the people they were supposed to serve. Their reaction to being treated without love is to act without mercy. Is this not is the defining characteristic of the lovelorn bureaucrat?

Sociologist Lewis Yablonsky, most famous for his work studying criminal gangs in New Jersey, proposed in his 1971 book *Robopaths* that people were beginning to lose the ability to think like human beings capable of independent thought and compassion. Yablonsky recognized that while technology might easily cause the destruction of the human race through nuclear or biological weapons, there was also a very real possibility that human beings might be eradicated through the all-encompassing, subtle power promised by technological productivity. Yablonsky theorized that a society dominated by machines and technology could have a damaging effect on human psychology.

Yablonsky argued that our society is developing what he called "robopathic tendencies." They are the teachers who willingly point out harmless students to school administrators, who are then subjected to brutal disciplinary measures. They are the principals who hand out suspensions to students who should perhaps be celebrated as heroes. They are the police officers who brutalize, fire upon and arrest citizens without any regard for their rights. They are the judges who hand out sentences knowing their rulings will make the situation even worse. They are the soldiers who, under orders, kill civilians, later claiming they were "only doing their jobs." The robopath has a hatred for natural life—for its variety, its exuberance, its individuality, joy and unpredictability. The robopath, like the citizens in *We* and the robots of *R.U.R.*, is not just compulsively conformist, but cannot tolerate nonconformity in anyone else. Where the human is understanding, loving and a ready to listen, the robopath sees the world in terms of impersonal absolutes.

Yablonsky writes that a world run by robopaths would be as deadly to humanity as any weapon of mass destruction:

> People may in a subtle fashion become robot-like in their interaction and become human robots or robopaths. This more insidious conclusion to the present course of action would be the silent disappearance of human interaction. In another kind of death, social death, people would be oppressively locked into robot-like interaction... In this context, the apocalypse would come in the form of people mouthing ahuman, regimented platitudes on a meaningless dead stage.

Yablonsky warned that the early symptoms of an emerging robopathic society were already apparent in 1971. Since then, this trend has become more pronounced. This robotlike inability to feel compassion, to act independently, and to see complex situations clearly is the main reason why our institutions' rule enforcers are increasingly unable to provide appropriate punishments for supposed infractions. To a considerable extent, we have already submitted to being ruled by robopaths.

In 1999 an article in the newspaper USA Today titled "Punish, don't destroy" recouned an incident in which Lisa Smith, an eighth-grade student, brought alcohol to school. She was punished with expulsion and "faces five months in a military-style boot camp." The article continues:

> Her parents agree she should have been punished. They took away all her privileges—telephone, TV, stereo— and reduced her room to just a desk and a bed.

> "Expulsion and boot camp? The punishment far exceeds the severity of the crime," says her father, Charlie Smith, a quality assurance inspector for an aerospace company.

> "Punish her, yes, but don't try to destroy her. She made one mistake. She is not a juvenile delinquent," says Ann Smith, her mother.

> Now she fears that her academic destiny will be permanently damaged by the severity of her punishment. "Just the term 'boot camp' scares me. I'm not a very physical person," she says.

The penalty was more severe than if she had been charged with the actual crime of underage possession of alcohol, which would have resulted in a ticket and a fine. But school officials said that they were just following the rules. "That's what school board policies specify," the robopathic Middle School Principal Steven Nauman who has a doctorate in education told reporters. "I have to agree with anything that's policy. My opinions are inconsequential. Citizens may not like speeding and no-parking signs, but we enforce them."[45]

The robopathic principal's deference to the written instructions was similar to that exhibited by a machine: if student breaks rule *x*, impose punishment *y*. Extenuating circumstances and past history of inappropriate behavior are not addressed in the school's written policies, and so they are ignored. Deference to the written rules is paramount, as though their mere existence is sufficient to justify an unjust act. The robopathic Dr. Nauman apparently sees students as objects to be acted upon, not as people with feelings and lives that matter. Even though he is entrusted with caring for children, he refuses to act compassionately and treats them the way a factory manager treats widgets. To the robopath, the system and its smooth functioning are more important than the people in it. If Nauman could acknowledge not only that the system was wrong, but that he had a personal moral responsibility to remedy that wrong, then he might stir himself to act justly. But he chose to hide behind rules as though they are the true governing force in society, rather than those like him, who are vested with the power to choose whether or not to apply them.

None of this is to say that it is unnecessary to have and to follow rules. Among many professions, there is an obvious need to adhere to rules, since most practitioners have neither the experience nor the expert knowledge to be able to rely on their own judgment. When specific expertise is lacking, placing trust in professionally respected figures is justified. In technical occupations, it is essential that employees act in a precise, predictable and consistent manner in order for the job to be completed efficiently and correctly. Jobs such as technicians, assembly line workers and air traffic controllers fall into this category. In the past, teachers have been largely exempt from such requirements and given ample latitude to instruct students in any way they saw fit. Once viewed as a creative and nurturing profession, teaching is becoming increasingly regi-

---

45 http://usatoday30.usatoday.com/educate/ednews3.htm

mented, with central planners even going as far as dictating specific rote responses to specific student questions. Teachers sensitive to this pressure may try to resist, but the trend is clearly to discourage individual initiative.

The main difference between a teacher and a technician is increasingly one of scale, not function. There are many more steps involved in teaching a child than are required by even the most technical job. Teachers have opportunities to show creativity and to vary their methods of teaching, but this is less true today than it was in the past. The drive for efficiency and the compulsion to exert central control has jeopardized teacher autonomy, and along with it the teachers' sense of self-worth. Coupled with increasing difficulties in teaching students who are easily distracted, stressed by problems at home, and poorly prepared for school makes the job that much harder. Teaching becomes a chore, not a calling, and subject to the same dehumanization as most other types of micromanaged occupations.

The relentless testing of both teachers and students, as well as collecting statistics on student behavior and various punishments, are intended to quantify the teaching process and to determine the most effective methods of control and instruction. The most visible of these include national criteria like Common Core and tests standardized at the state level. The stated purpose of all this data gathering is to improve the accountability of teachers and their schools, but the real purpose is to homogenize student learning so that it can be scientifically measured, understood and managed by machines. The unintended consequence is that the feeling of being constantly monitored and evaluated is suffocating for both students and teachers. Teaching is a nuanced art that cannot be reduced to numbers on a spreadsheet but this won't stop the bureaucrats from trying exactly that.

The effect on teachers has been deeply demoralizing. According to a 2012 MetLife survey of teachers, job satisfaction among principals is at the lowest level in a decade (59 percent). The number of teachers who describe their job as very satisfying is down from 62 percent in 2008 to 39 percent in 2012. The survey also reports that the number of teachers experiencing stress several days a week or more is up to 51 percent from 36 percent in 1985.[46]

In a well-publicized resignation letter, one social studies teacher claimed that his profession no longer existed:

> My profession is being demeaned by a pervasive atmosphere of distrust, dictating that teachers cannot be permitted to develop and administer their own quizzes and tests (now titled as generic "assessments") or grade their own students' examinations. The development of plans, choice of lessons and the materials to be employed are increasingly expected to be common to all teachers in a given subject. This approach not only strangles creativity, it smothers the development of critical thinking in our students and assumes a one-size-fits-all mentality more appropriate to the assembly line than to the classroom. Teacher planning time has also now been so greatly eroded by a constant need to "prove up" our worth... that there is little time for us to carefully critique student work, engage in informal intellectual discussions with our students and colleagues, or conduct research and seek personal improvement through independent study. We have become increasingly evaluation and not knowledge driven. Process has become our most important product, to twist a phrase from corporate America, which seems doubly appropriate to this case.[47]

---

46 https://www.metlife.com/assets/cao/foundation/MetLife-Teacher-Survey-2012.pdf
47 http://www.dailykos.com/story/2014/11/11/1343935/-Teacher-s-resignation-letter-My-profession-no-longer-exists

Since teachers and school administrators are not robots but humans and have human emotions, the inevitable result of their frustration is violence against children—expressed in cryptic, underhanded, bureaucratic ways. Yablonsky's theory helps to explain the willingness of teachers and administrators to impose harsh punishments, occasionally with apparent glee:

"People unable to act out their spontaneity and creativity develop repressed, venomous pockets of hostility," Yablonsky writes. "Many bureaucrats often have an acceptable structure for ventilating their hostility on other people. They can use the rules to deny others things they desire (e.g. 'The rules do not permit...' 'We regret we cannot deliver...' etc.)"

Examples of bureaucratic aggression are endless, but here is one that epitomizes the problem. Angela Prattis went out of her way to feed poor children in her neighborhood in Chester County, Pennsylvania. Through donations coordinated by local church groups, every afternoon she fed up to 60 kids in a gazebo on her property. Local news reported that Prattis provided weekly reports and received regular visits from state workers. The program even received funding directly from the state's department of education. But in the summer of 2012 city officials fined Prattis $600, and said that she would continue to be fined every day she fed the children because she had failed to observe zoning ordinances which prohibit handing out food, even for free, in a residential zone.

When Prattis asked what she could do to allow the program to stay open, township officials told her to shut it down. Township Council Chairman Stanley Kester said: "She wants us to bypass or exonerate her from the zoning hearing. She just doesn't want to pay to do things the right way... We can't just start exempting everyone from our laws. If you do one, you've got to do everybody."[48]

---

48 http://www.theblaze.com/stories/2012/08/14/im-not-stopping-penn-woman-faces-600-daily-fine-for-feeding-hungry-children/

With the help of lawyers working pro bono Prattis had a vacant lot across from her property rezoned as a public park and continued feeding the kids from there.

Can the lives of American bureaucrats and rule-followers be so tortuous that hungry children become viable targets for their simmering outrage? Or is the pressure from authorities higher up the hierarchy so great that lowly rule enforcers have no choice but to comply? Whatever the cause, the streak of official sadism is unmistakable.

This official sadism prays on the weak and the poor. In recent years there has been a move toward what critics call "criminalizing homelessness." City ordinances have outlawed "homeless camps," sitting on sidewalks and sleeping in public. Police can now jail the homeless for being homeless and people who feed the homeless for feeding them. San Antonio, Texas is one of the harshest cities when it comes to feeding the dispossessed. It recently fined a woman $2,000 for failing to use a proper vehicle when transporting food. Joan Cheever, founder of the nonprofit food truck, the Chow Train, had a permit to feed the homeless in a city park, but did not use The Chow Train food truck to serve the food. Cheever told the San Antonio Express News: "We cook dinner in the truck and then we put it in health-department-approved catering equipment, like every caterer or restaurant delivery service in this town, and then serve it. And [the police officer] said, 'You can't do that.'"[49]

For her part, Cheever had no hard feelings toward the police who issued her the ticket. "I'm just sorry for the four members of the SAPD bike patrol," She said. "I'm so sorry because they looked very uncomfortable. I thanked them for their service but I'm sorry that the city put them in this position."[50]

49 http://www.expressnews.com/news/news_columnists/gilbert_garcia/article/City-s-homeless-crackdown-reaches-a-new-low-6193914.phpv
50 http://www.sacurrent.com/Blogs/archives/2015/04/14/good-samaritan-holding-vigil-at-maverick-park-where-sapd-ticketed-her-for-

Critics charge that the city's intent is to drive the homeless from the sections of the city where tourists are likely to congregate. While the city's decisions can be condemned for their lack of human compassion, the decision to hand out a $2,000 ticket to someone feeding the homeless rests on the police who were presumably ordered to issue the fine. That the justification for the fine rests on what amounts to a creative use of a technicality is especially telling: there was some sort of sinister intelligence behind the act, and it is not exactly human.

This kind of behavior is rational, but this rationality is also extremely short-sighted. Often, robopathic institutions like governments and corporations make decisions that make sense from some very limited viewpoint, but are actually destructive of society's wider needs. Bureaucratic systems are designed to solve problems, and sometimes to improve efficiency, but without the influence of a benevolent, or at least a benign human intelligence they can have the opposite effect, making problems worse.

At times it seems that no problem is too small for some bureaucracy to run with and make it into a huge boondoggle. In anthropologist Edward Hall's 1976 book *Beyond Culture*, he describes a story of a wild dog that lived happily on the small, otherwise uninhabited island of Ruffle Bar, which is just off the coast of Brooklyn and Long Island. The dog, nicknamed "The King of Ruffle Bar," seemed to be in good health and had sustained itself for about two years. Some well-meaning person heard about the dog and reported it to the local ASPCA. That's when the bureaucratic wheels began to spin.

Officials became obsessively preoccupied with capturing the dog, even going as far as using a helicopter to hover over the island daily, at a cost of thousands of dollars per flight. The dog continued to evade police, eventually attracting a nationwide audience as the police continued in vain to try to capture him. The New York Times reported that the dog "looked in

---

feeding-homeless-people

good shape." Indeed, the police had been aware of the dog for at least two years and had been content to leave him on the is - land. "Why don't they leave the dog alone?" one officer asked. "The dog is as happy as a pig in a puddle."

Representatives for the ASPCA said: "When we catch the dog, we will have it examined by a vet, and if it is in good health, we will find a happy home for it." The fact that the dog already had an entire island to itself didn't matter because the setting was not under their bureaucratic control. Hall wrote:

> The ASPCA became obsessed with capturing the dog. Once triggered, the ASPCA involved the police with a remorseless, mindless persistence that is too terrify- ingly characteristic of bureaucracies once they are acti- vated...
>
> The delusional aspects of this story have to do with the institutionalized necessity to control *everything*, and the widely accepted notion that the bureaucrat knows what is best—never for a moment does she doubt the validity of the bureaucratic solution. It is also not just a little bit insane, or at least indicative of our incapacity to order priorities with any common sense, to spend thousands of dollars on helicopters, gasoline, and salaries for the sole purpose of bureaucratic neatness.

A bureaucracy, once activated, can be very dangerous be - cause reason cannot constrain it in its quest for uniformity. Hall notes that this is primarily a western problem, not one shared the world over:

"We in the west are alienated from ourselves and from na- ture," he writes. "We labor under a number of delusions, one of which is that life makes sense, that we are sane. We persist in this view despite massive evidence to the contrary."

Slightly insane seems like a fair assessment of ASPCA be - havior in this instance. But other outbursts of bureaucratic insanity, which often result in the criminalization of young children, the murder of innocent people and the violation of individual rights on a nationwide level, this epidemic of irrational thought and abusive behavior no longer seems more than slightly insane.

5. A World Without Meaning

Rampant bureaucracy has done more than simply suppress our autonomy. It has helped us make great strides in science, engineering and medicine, but it has obliterated our sense of meaning and purpose and has failed to provide a story that has *personal* meaning. Scientific control of human beings has excelled primarily because it has enabled us to exploit our environment in new ways. But it has trapped us in a world of technology, organizational systems, and rules we can never hope to understand fully. Machines have grown so complicated that —to paraphrase Arthur C. Clarke—they have become indistinguishable from magic. Science does not prove itself through personal experience or by satisfying a psychological need, but rather through regular miracles—the jet airliner, the GPS receiver, the cell phone—which are readily visible to everyone and quickly become mundane, engendering belief but not faith.

For the average person, these regular miracles prove the existence of a new god—whose only commandment is *consume more*. Experts provide us with answers that leave us floating in a sea of unconnected, unfathomable facts. We can neither grapple with our lack of understanding nor can we effectively rebel against it, because we lack expertise. By weakening our certainty about almost everything except the need to *consume more*, the experts have turned us into easy prey for those who seek to define our meaning for us by seducing us with a wide variety of standardized products and services. And as long as we do get to *consume more*, we are happy to let the bureaucrats tell us exactly what we must do.

The military

In his various works, including *Technics and Civilization* and *The Reinvention of the Megamachine*, Lewis Mumford noted that the First World War was a large-scale bureaucratic operation. In fact, any sufficiently huge bureaucracy can be viewed as a small-scale military operation. Since the military is an inherently dehumanizing force that takes civilians and fashions them into efficient killers, this perspective warrants greater examination.

Compared to today's, earlier systems of military command and control were rather limited. Lacking the necessary communications technology, militaries of old were unable to fully robotize the individuals within them, and had to allow for individual initiative. Even the lower levels of command structure operated with a great deal of autonomy.

At the dawn of the modern era this began to change. Monarchies faded away and human sovereigns were replaced by a sovereign nation state—powered in large part by coal and other forms of plentiful, inexpensive energy. Unlike the human sovereign, the nation state has no physical form and only exists in the minds of its subjects. The major shift toward establishing a government capable of employing micro-level social controls picked up speed substantially during the two World Wars, when effective state propaganda began to rope in previously free-thinking peoples.

Consider Albert Speer, Minister of Armaments and War Production for Nazi Germany during World War II. During his war crimes trial at Nuremberg he said:

Hitler's dictatorship... made the complete use of all technical means for domination of its own country. Through technical devices like the radio and the loudspeaker, 80 million people were deprived of independent thought. It was thereby possible to subject them to the will of one man... Earlier dictators needed highly qualified assistants even at the lowest level—men who could think and act independently. The totalitarian system in the period of modern technical development can dispense with such men; thanks to modern methods of communication, it is possible to mechanize the lower leadership. As a result of this there has arisen the new type of the uncritical recipient of orders.[51]

While Speer insisted that he was not an ideologue and claimed ignorance of the Holocaust (a claim that seemed implausible to many) he followed his orders, indicating that it was not merely the "lower leadership" that was being micromanaged, but that even he, in a high position of authority, was subject to pressures that challenged his sense of right and wrong. He admitted as much both at the Nuremberg trials and later upon his release from prison in the 1960s. In his book *Infiltration* he asks: "What would have happened if Hitler had asked me to make decisions that required the utmost hardness?... How far would I have gone?... If I had occupied a different position, to what extent would I have ordered atrocities if Hitler had told me to do so?"

Centralized command and control systems may give military machines a short-term destructive edge over disorganized civilians and the rest of nature, but such centralized power is also their greatest weakness. Because all meaningful decisions are made at the top, questions regarding the wisdom of those decisions are often ignored, corrective actions are not taken and errors are allowed to compound. As military machines grow larger and add more and more layers of hierarchy with a

---

51 Aldous Huxley, *Brave New World Revisited*

bigger and bigger disconnect between the view from the top and the facts on the ground, this tendency becomes more and more pronounced.

It must be remembered what makes this military-bureaucratic edifice temporarily possible: it is cheap and abundant energy from fossil fuels. The military-industrial nation state is in large part a product of the efficiency gains obtained by burning first coal, then oil and natural gas, and it follows that the current global superpower is largely the result of cheap and plentiful oil. The US military is the single largest consumer of petroleum products in the world; without them, its ability to project military power around the world would swiftly vanish. Alternatives to oil, which is becoming progressively more energy-intensive and expensive to produce, have proven to be elusive, and with them the dreams of global government.

"Every totalitarian system brings its own enemies," Mumford writes, "to the very degree the system is self-sealed—incapable of self-criticism and self-correction." He writes that Stalin's stubborn unwillingness to see Hitler's preparations for invading almost cost USSR the war. Meanwhile, Hitler continued to kill off large parts of the German population which could have been used as soldiers or laborers in the fight against the numerically superior Allies. Despite its efficiency in carrying out specific objectives, the military-bureaucratic machine is not capable of taking on board alternative viewpoints that might prevent it from self-destruction. There is, it would seem, a trade-off between the centralization of authority and the ability to carefully craft decisions capable of compensating for unforeseen and unintended consequences.

Questions about more ethereal, non-quantifiable values, such as the value of peace over war, often go completely unexamined because unhindered human lives, the unmolested natural world, and concepts such as freedom from militarism do not translate to any meaningful metric that the military machine can analyze and translate into actions. The concept of the sacred—a respect for all living things, a mysterious and largely unexplainable respect for the world beyond human desires—this is what can make us good custodians of the natural realm on which our survival depends. And this is what a military machine cannot value or even acknowledge.

Military machines cannot place a value on taboos. Instead they value what are called "technics." Technics are the quantifiable values of reality. Munitions used, dollars spent, resources seized from the enemy, enemies killed and structures destroyed—these can all be weighted and assessed, while non-quantifiable concepts such as human dignity, sense of well-being and fulfillment are discarded as inconsequential, if they are ever considered at all.

Jacques Ellul

Jacques Ellul described these values in his 1954 book *The Technological Society*:

> Technique worships nothing, respects nothing. It has a single role: to strip off externals, to bring everything to light, and by rational use to transform everything into means. More than science, which limits itself to explaining the 'how,' technique desacralizes because it demonstrates (by evidence and not by reason, through use and not through books) that mystery does not exist. Science brings to the light of day everything man had believed sacred. Technique takes possession of it and enslaves it. The sacred cannot resist. Science penetrates to the great depths of the sea to photograph the unknown fish of the deep. Technique captures them, hauls

them up to see if they are edible...[52]

Consider America's war in Vietnam, which was probably the United States' largest military boondoggle (to date, although Afghanistan is now its longest-running one) and arguably the largest imperial war of the 20th century. At that time, Secretary of Defense Robert McNamara attempted to apply statistical methods which he had taught as a professor at Harvard Business School to America's military campaigns in Southeast Asia. Logic and mathematics which he learned as an economics major at the University of California at Berkeley produced a fundamental shift in how he viewed the potential for productive capacity. In his 1996 biography, he wrote: "To this day, I see quantification as a revelation."[53] He saw in the certainty of numbers a neutral construct that could be used beneficially: to lessen poverty, shorten war, and increase government efficiency. "Running the Department of Defense is not different from running the Ford Motor Company or the Catholic Church, for that matter," McNamara said in 1962. "Once you get to a certain scale, it's all the same."[54]

Robert McNamara

In his book on war crimes in Vietnam, *Kill Anything That Moves*, researcher Nick Turse describes the military's obsession with warfare as a science that could be understood and conquered through numerical analysis. He wrote:

52 Jacques Ellul, *The Technological Society*, 1954, p. 142
53 *In Retrospect: The Tragedy and Lessons of Vietnam*, p. 6
54 *On Effective Leadership: Across Domains, Cultures, and Eras*, p. 42

[McNamara] brought to the Pentagon a corps of "whiz kids' and "computer jockeys' whose job was to transform military establishment into a corporatized system that could, as the political commentator Tom Engelhardt put it, "be managed in the same 'scientific' and 'efficient' manner as a business." McNamara seemed almost to mimic the computers that he and his staff so fervently believed in. He relied on numbers to convey reality and, like a machine, processed whatever information he was given with exceptional speed, making instant choices and not worrying that such rapid-fire decision making might lead to grave mistakes. McNamara and his national security technocrats were sure that, given enough data, warfare could be made completely rational, comprehensible, and controllable. And they never looked back.

Progress was not inherently destructive, McNamara argued. In fact it was more likely to be constructive. In Vietnam, progress was largely measured by enemy body count, both in absolute terms and measured against US casualties. The result was an astounding 3.8 million Vietnamese fatal and non-fatal casualties against just over 300,000 US casualties.[55] Despite the imbalance in friendly to hostile casualties, the US still lost the war, proving that one-dimensional statistics are often an incomplete measure of success.

Historians have tried to calculate the number of people who have died due to war in the 20th century, resulting in wildly different figures ranging from over 100 million to just over 200 million if you include man-made famines and other atrocities resulting from internal oppression from national governments. Go back further and figures become much more difficult to pin down, so it is debatable that deaths per capita have increased as technology and social controls have enabled greater and more centrally directed devastation.

55 *Kill Anything That Moves*, by Nick Turse;
http://www.nationalvietnamveteransfoundation.org/statistics.htm

Measuring deaths is different from quantifying other products of power, especially when they result from psychological pressure, which is now employed on a global scale. After all, the goal of militaries and aggressive governments is not to kill their opponents but to conquer them. Conquest through psychological means (i.e., the lure of consumerism, financial benefits of debt-based capitalism for the elite and the spread of other "cultural values") can be almost entirely covert.

Later in life, McNamara did admit that "rationality alone will not save us." While he was talking about the potential for nuclear war, the principle would seem to apply to all government activities. Still, McNamara was to the end of his life a believer in quantifiable methods of control. When asked by documentary film maker Errol Morris in 2003 who was responsible for the Vietnam War, McNamara said: "It's the President's responsibility."

McNamara clearly had a brilliant mind for using quantifiable data for constructive (or destructive) ends, but he was completely blind to non-quantifiable values and to his own moral responsibility in enabling the killing machine. In the end McNamara resorted to the same defense the Nazis at Nuremberg —they were not to blame because they were following orders. "[In] an era of world war," Randolph Bourne wrote in 1918, "statesmen are proving as blind and helpless as the manipulated masses." Anyone can fall into a trap of purely rationalistic decision-making, while ignoring all that which cannot be measured.

Torture

When bureaucracies *want* to inflict lasting psychological harm, they can do so with great ease, completely eliminating people's ability to resist.

One of the arguments posed by classic philosophers is that it is impossible to deny someone their moral autonomy. There is always a way out of being co-opted by the bureaucratic machine, be it through desertion or extreme pacifism, provided you are willing to disregard the consequences. The slave becomes free the moment he wishes to do so. Even if the consequence of freedom is death, the slave still has the option dying with his principles intact. The philosophical stance is that betrayal of one's principles is always and everywhere a free choice.

Sadly, there are exceptions. It isn't just propaganda that assails our free will, but the scientifically informed methods which can make our bodies and minds submit to pressure against our will. During the Cold War, new methods of mind control were fashioned that do not require even a modicum of consent. The use of fear as a weapon of mass control has been widely discussed and studied by both psychologists and politicians. Fear makes principled decision-making difficult and renders crowd psychology predictable. From the perspective of a science-minded dictator, if citizens' actions are predictable, then they can be controlled. Still, fear cannot be sustained for long periods of time. Also, not everyone will respond to fear in a predictable way. Others will see through the use of fear as a cynical attempt at control and look for ways to subvert it. It is suitable for mass use, but fear cannot be relied on for controlling the actions of a single, strong-minded individual in a precise, predictable way.

Among the most widely used (but also the least reliable) forms of control is the use of mass hypnosis through television and radio. Hypnotic inductions through the radio are common. The television is a hypnotic device by design, radiating light in such a way as to put the brain into a passive, "alpha" state of activity, just below that of full, normal consciousness. When a subject is in the alpha state, broadcast messages can partially bypass the conscious mind and directly penetrate the subconscious. Hypnotic therapy can be used to empower people by aligning their conscious desires with their naturally more hesitant and fearful subconscious. Students of this particular kind of mind discipline can eliminate the urge to smoke, boost self-confidence, get people to stop biting their nails and more. Hypnosis is used in advertising because it does make consumers more likely to act on their desires, especially if they believe that the desire to buy a product originates from within them. Overall, hypnosis does function as a form of control, albeit a weak one.

Far less covert, but also far more effective, is the use of sensory deprivation, where a subject is isolated from all sensation. At its most extreme, this state can be used as a method of indoctrination that can only be called torture: pain, dread, disorientation, drugs, humiliation, and more are brought to bear to tear down the mind's defenses. The subject may be blindfolded, placed in a soundproof room with a constant temperature, with arms and legs constrained. Ideally, toes and fingers will also be separated by cotton or otherwise immobilized. An apparatus will be placed in the mouth to limit tongue motion. Finally, the subject may be suspended in room temperature water to limit the feeling of gravity. In this state, the subject has no senses at all. All experience that remains is the experience of the mind. While you might think that this would make the mind stronger, the effect is the exact opposite: quickly, a sense of self breaks down. At this point, all stimulus the subject does receive takes on extra weight. The messages become extremely powerful because the subject is less able to distinguish messages coming from within him and the messages being fed to him by others.

Sleep deprivation (subjecting those under interrogation to strobe lights and white noise) and force feeding are common tools of the modern torturer. Within boundaries, torturers can experiment to see what works. The less visible the harm done to detainees, the less likely is the action to be deemed torture by military doctors.

Policies which promote the use of torture have a perilous quality to them. Since they operate under the premise that a small amount of torture is beneficial, it follows that more torture will produce more positive results. Lawyer and university professor Phillipe Sands notes that within a military structure, cruelty is infectious, and one might argue that this is true in a society as a whole. He said:

> Once you open the door to a little bit of cruelty, people will believe that more cruelty is a good thing. And once the dogs are unleashed, it's impossible to put them back on. And that's the basis for the belief amongst a lot of people in the military that the interrogation techniques basically slipped from Guantanamo to Iraq, and to Abu Ghraib.[56]

The big disadvantage of torture, and violence in general, is that it leaves the victim crippled—mentally, physically or both. But the bureaucracy needs people to work in its service. Such violent force cannot be used against the population as a whole primarily because it is highly inefficient, while efficiency is paramount to the smooth functioning of the bureaucratic machine. Also, sooner or later the widespread use of force shatters the illusion that the government is looking out for the public interest. The greater its use of force, the more the state is forced to admit that it is losing control.

Civilization's Death Instinct

In one of his final HBO specials *Life is Worth Losing*, comedian George Carlin explained that, in a sense, destruction gave him joy. He said:

> I have absolutely no sympathy for human beings whatsoever. None. And no matter what kind of problem humans are facing, whether it's natural or man-made, I always hope it gets worse.

---

56 http://www.pbs.org/moyers/journal/05092008/watch2.html

Don't you? Don't you have a part of you that secretly hopes everything gets worse? When you see a big fire on TV, don't you hope it spreads? Don't you hope it gets completely out of control and burns down six counties? You don't root for the firemen do you? I mean I don't want them to get hurt or nothing, but I don't want them to put out my fire. That's my fire—that's nature showing off and having fun. I like fires.

Sigmund Freud

He goes on in this vein for quite some time. Disaster, when it concerns the destruction of mankind's creations, makes a fun spectacle. Film audiences that ate up the disaster flicks of the 1970s would agree. Consider 1974's *The Towering Inferno*, in which man's arrogance turns a skyscraper into a pile of smoking rubble. The 135-story building symbolizes, according to the movie's own script, "a kind of shrine to all the bullshit in the world."

In *Civilization and its Discontents*, Sigmund Freud wrote that humans had a "death instinct"—an unconscious desire for death that is expressed as outward aggressiveness. This aggressiveness, he concluded, was "the greatest impediment to civilization," but one that a cultural superego or a cultural conscience could limit. We are taught to suppress this urge to destroy and to feel guilty about our obvious love of destruction, but the collapse of buildings and things in a typical disaster film is too exciting. According to any number of hackneyed plot lines, disaster strikes because a powerful elite wouldn't listen to the film's plucky band of heroes. On the rare occasion when forests are leveled and animals die, this is presented as a tragedy—because animals and forests represent an ideal—a vision of the world to which we should all want to return. Nobody wants to watch a disaster film with lots of dead cute furry animals! We pay to see the White House destroyed by a giant flying saucer, or the Empire State Building smashed by an asteroid, or even whole cities cinematically obliterated hundreds of times over, as long as no cute puppies or kittens are harmed as a result.

During the Cold War, demands that we launch a first strike nuclear attack against the Soviet Union, while not mainstream, were common enough within the military establishment and among the public to warrant concern. What could cause people to crave such massive, suicidal destruction? Theologian Thomas Merton recalled receiving a letter from a woman in the 1960s, right around the time of the Cuban Missile Crisis. In it, she petitioned the monk for prayers that the US would soon launch a nuclear attack against the Soviet Union and its 200 million residents. Pleading with him, she wrote, "We cannot stand it any longer."

Thomas Merton

In 2003, Comedian Julian Morrow asked a dozen or so random people who the United States should bomb next. Most answered, Iran, North Korea or Russia, but a few mentioned Cuba, Italy and even Canada. One individual even said we should bomb France, because "They were not our allies [during the Iraq War]." None of the dozen or so shown in the interview said that we shouldn't bomb anyone.[57]

In 2015, decades after the Cold War ended, a videographer in California asked some random pedestrians to sign a petition urging President Obama to launch a preemptive nuclear strike on Russia, "to show Putin who is boss" and, amazingly, they signed it![58] When in response the television channel RT sent a representative into the streets of Moscow to get Muscovites to sign a petition to nuclear-bomb the US, most of them refused to sign and instead questioned his sanity. Apparently, Russians lack this death wish. So, what makes Americans different?[59]

Americans have a profound sense of what Hegel called "negative identity." A society with a negative identity defines itself not by what it is but by what it is not, and is always on the lookout for new and fashionable enemies from which to differentiate themselves in superficial ways. Sigmund Freud got at the same thing with his "doctrine of small differences." It is much easier to hate that which you closely resemble, focusing on minor differences and projecting everything you dislike about yourself onto the other, than to find reasons to hate that which is entirely unfamiliar. A negative identity can be psychologically fortifying and justify murder, invasions and even genocide. But while a society built on a negative identity may be willing to die fighting a made-up enemy, it can't find anything worth living for.

Francis Fukuyama famously, and most embarrassingly, argued that after the collapse of the Soviet Union global capitalism emerged dominant, unchallenged, and—for the near future at least—sustainable. The world had reached "the end of history." He was not alone: French social theorist Jean Baudrillard agreed that there was indeed an end to combating narratives, but also an end to the idea of progress itself. What had

---

57 https://www.youtube.com/watch?v=qUYm50jQscw
58 https://www.youtube.com/watch?v=CNr5czZKEdk
59 http://on.rt.com/84vc0g

emerged in its place was rather the absence of any universal story or meaning. For a time, national narratives that had helped to define and defend the nation state during its prime had evaporated without enemies to threaten it. The existential strain which had been masked by the fear and hatred of Communism had resurfaced, leading some to suggest that the United States needed an enemy to provide itself with an identity.

Of course, this theory rests on the questionable assumption that the United States isn't just some mechanical social invention. But we know that the US Government's motivations are material, not psychological. It has a desire to sustain growth and to maintain its hegemonic power, which was for a time almost unchecked. It pursues policies in support of these goals, but stops short of triggering an unwinnable nuclear conflict. However, the people within the government are not so single-minded. The beleaguered bureaucrat is absolutely desperate to come up with an explanation for the mundane stress of individual existence. It is this morass of individual meaningless that makes sudden global war more likely.

In our failed search for identity, negative or otherwise, many of us become like the monster in Mary Shelly's *Frankenstein*—hopeful that death will finally give us with rest. In the final chapter of the novel the monster, having taken his revenge upon his creator, realizes that he no longer has any reason for living:

> I shall die, and what I now feel be no longer felt. Soon these burning miseries will be extinct. I shall ascend my funeral pile triumphantly and exult in the agony of the torturing flames. The light of that conflagration will fade away; my ashes will be swept into the sea by the winds. My spirit will sleep in peace, or if it thinks, it will not surely think thus. Farewell.

When an individual is faced with a meaningless existence, mass annihilation becomes subconsciously desirable. Enforced uniformity, individual meaninglessness and mass destruction come as a package. Destruction becomes therapeutic, but it's a therapy devised by madmen which, when matched with nuclear weapons, may result in the entire human race reclassifying itself as collateral damage.

To a dehumanized bureaucrat deprived of identity or purpose, an atomic wasteland may indeed be the image of peace. Perhaps the entire military-industrial complex, and all the violence it unleashes on the world, is, at the individual level, a cry for help.

> "From adolescence to retirement, each 24-hour cycle repeats the same shattering bombardment, like bullets hitting a window: mechanical repetition, time-which-is-money, submission to bosses, boredom, exhaustion. From the butchering of youth's energy to the gaping wound of old age, life cracks in every direction under the blows of forced labor. Never before has a civilization reached such a degree of contempt for life; never before has a generation, drowned in mortification, felt such a rage to live."
>
> —Raoul Vaneigem, *The Revolution of Everyday Life*

6. The Education of a Robopath

The "bureaucratic personality"—a term coined by Max Weber for the ideal worker in an industrial society—is essential for the proper functioning of complex bureaucracies. We've called them bureaucrats, rule enforcers, robopaths.

Narrow, absolutist, robotlike thinking may be common in today's society, but people are not born thinking this way. Psychologically normal children do not act with such reverence to rules that they would knowingly harm someone else for the sake of obeying a rule. It's true, some children are born psychopaths who care only about themselves, but psychopaths have no respect for rules either. Children start out with no commitment to order, absolutism, conformity, nor any desire to put other people "in their place." Such phenomena are limited to adults. Children are actually more likely to point out the irrationality of certain rules.

The institutional molding period normally begins during adolescence, but in the US it has been occurring earlier and earlier. Children are thrust into institutional settings, away  from their families, starting at a very young age. The disintegration of the nuclear family and the needs of parents who are working two or three jobs make day care essential. Child daycare centers are by their nature more controlling and more efficient as a matter of necessity, since many children must be observed and taken care of simultaneously by a small staff. However, they are not a substitute for traditional parenting, which is normally much more intimate and loving. This is not to say that all parents are great and all daycare centers terrible, but good institutions cannot match the instinctual, unconditional love of good parents who are regularly present in their children's lives.

Max Weber

Politicians who are keen to find more ways to micromanage schools and increase testing sometimes refer to children as "investments." To safeguard society's "investments," children are placed in ever more controlled settings. This process continues through the adolescent years and well into adulthood. By the time young adults are ready to enter the workforce, they are already used to dealing with apathetic adults who don't care about them as individuals, and don't even bother to feign interest the way some adults may have when they were little. They are taught not to expect much from other people, nor give much of themselves to others. This is called professionalism, but it is more accurate to describe it as alienation.

They are well on their way to becoming robopaths.

Robopaths are different from psychopaths. Psychopaths also lack empathy and sometimes fake emotions to get what they want, but they also have no respect for social norms. A robopath, on the other hand, is a stickler for social norms. Robopaths are ultra-conformists. Their sense of self-worth is built on obeying rules compulsively and with great precision. Because they fit into society's vision of acceptable behavior, robopaths are difficult to spot except in situations where their inhumanity becomes apparent. Where no rules are present, or where rules specifically encourage sympathetic behavior, robopaths may be able to mimic feelings of concern and seem sincere.

The degree to which someone is inflexible and alienated can vary wildly. Some robopaths may be able to act humane in most situations, only making a strict commitment to the rules under certain circumstances or in certain settings. Many people can be reasoned with or shamed into acting humanely, but this often takes enormous effort, because many robopaths sincerely believe that their actions are justified as long as they follow the rules. Others' capacity for empathy may have atrophied from disuse. They may only be capable of ritualized expressions of sympathy and shallow socializing, and cannot be reached with an emotional appeal, which they would see as ridiculous.

Robopaths are rarely shunned by society. Their commitment to enforcing and obeying written rules protects them from official sanction. When challenged, they are self-righteous and certain of the morality of their position. Their professionalism and dispassionate demeanor are widely seen as a sign of maturity. Those who show a reverence to the rules may be rewarded with positions of greater authority and symbols of status. They have an automatic sense of purpose—which is simply to be promoted within the bureaucracy. Their identity is reinforced by their level of commitment to following the rules. As a result of all this positive reinforcement, they are often more at ease with themselves and with their social roles than those who question the rules and attempt to use their own judgment. Robopaths proliferate within society because their behavior is accepted and rewarded.

How does someone turn into a robopath? If we examine the pressures of contemporary family life, school and office work, we can find clues as to the origin of the bureaucratic personality and its delusions, but we also need to consider the wider sociological context. How were these personalities initially shaped? At what point did they begin to identify their own self-esteem with the proper, perfect enforcement of the rules? At what point did future school administrators begin to feel that it is morally acceptable to ignore, and in some cases even to despise, the emotional pleas of children?

Dr. Alexander Lowen, the founder of "body psychotherapy," part of a field of study called bioenergetics, argues that psychological conditions have a direct relationship with the body. He notes that when a person makes a habit of continually *repressing* an action, feelings can become *suppressed* and cannot be felt:

> The suppression of impulses is not a conscious or selective process like the act of holding back their expression. It is the result of continual holding back of expression until that holding back becomes a habitual mode and an unconscious body attitude. In effect, the area of the body that would be involved in the expression of the impulse is deadened... In a desperate maneuver to survive, one deadens the whole body. If this deadening goes far enough, it produces the schizoid personality.[60]

Lowen likens this tendency to a crying child unable to find his mother. At first, the child's cries are intense, continuing until exhaustion. Later the child may cry again, but progres-

---

60 Alexander Lowen, *Depression and the Body*, p. 80-81

sively weaker every time. Eventually, if the child still cannot find the mother, depression sets in and the child becomes deadened to all feeling.

Or imagine a worker who is continually angered by her boss. The natural reaction might be to strike out verbally or physically, but because that would be considered unprofessional behavior, this action is *repressed*. When the action is repressed habitually, the anger becomes *suppressed*. But the underlying emotion doesn't go away; instead, the worker struggles to find new, socially acceptable ways to express it.

The alienated worker becomes deadened to her own desires. By continually denying her discomfort, she becomes detached from her emotions, deflated and depressed, but no longer able to find the source of her suffering. But she can relieve her inner tension by taking it out on others in socially acceptable ways. For the alienated bureaucrat, this target is often the public she is supposed to serve.

While the public suffers, the family tends to be spared. The alienated bureaucrat deals with the conflicting demands of work and home through *compartmentalization*, which is used to create two separate value systems. People who have compartmentalized their values act radically differently in different settings. An alienated worker may be sincerely compassionate or caring at home and with her neighbors and eager to engage in exploitative, aggressive behavior at work, ignoring such inconsistencies within her character to the point that she is not even conscious of them. In this way, an alienated bureaucrat can remain faithful to her expectations at work while maintaining a positive self-image.

Yablonsky suggests the development of robopathic tendencies begins when children first enter school, in what Mark Ames calls the "post diaper rat-race." There they are taught to observe time constraints more closely, meet teachers' commands with precision, and obey commands that often seem arbitrary. Unable to challenge the ruling dynamic of their lives, children either adapt or get labeled as disobedient or disruptive. They either find satisfaction within the constraints they are given or they become social outcasts. Thus, submissive ways of thinking are instilled starting at a young age and appear broadly throughout society.

Children tend to be far more curious in their earliest years, exploring and playing without regard to cultural norms. But to progress to the next stage in their lives, children must absorb the culture—which, in a regimented, industrialized society, means obedience to rules they may not understand, as well as displaying restrained, introverted behavior. It also means a ban on most forms of physical violence, but widespread and unacknowledged, psychological violence. Children are forced to accept uncompassionate behavior and indifferent attitudes in adults who are already trapped by society's bureaucratic control systems. The result, writes psychologist R. D. Laing, is that "by the time the new human being is fifteen or so, we are left with a being like ourselves, a half-crazed creature more or less adjusted to a mad world. This is normality in our present age."[61]

* * *

The profit motive, which we must all obey if we wish to remain employed, promotes exploitative values. It doesn't allow us to see ourselves as part of nature, or even of a human community. It allows us to treat the world, and each other, as mere objects. The tree provides wood, oil provides energy, children produce good test scores, corporations produce shareholder value, countries produce GDP growth, and all of these objects exist merely to serve their owners. If something can't be made to serve, it has no value.

The range of what we can set aside as inherently valuable or sacred is steadily shrinking. We identify only with our own

---

61 R.D. Laing, *The Politics of Experience*, p. 58

immediate families and, if we are lucky, a few very close friends. Only they qualify as being really "one of us" and worth protecting without there being a profit motive. Pretty much everything else, including our colleagues, other people's children, and all of nature, are basically alien to us. Since they are not inherently valuable, it is acceptable to act aggressively toward them and to ignore their emotional needs while concentrating on our own. If you see other individuals as not inherently valuable but merely as objects, then they can be made part of any commercial activity without reservation: hired, fired, bought, sold, coerced or abandoned.

To put it very plainly, people within a corporate environment cannot love. They are forbidden from acting in a way that is truly compassionate because that would get in the way of the bureaucratic machine's goals. If you did truly love your coworkers, your students, your employees, and saw them suffer at the hands of the system, your conscience would force you to rebel against the system. And so you play it safe and cultivate an atmosphere of professional detachment, remaining unemotional and robotlike toward the people around you. In order to be able to keep their distance, people carefully script their interactions along safe lines. People can ask questions about each other's lives, their goals and struggles, superficial health problems. They can also observe birthdays and other joyous occasions. But none of this can be allowed to get serious: professionalism requires that if a person is judged to be detrimental to the company's interest and is fired, colleagues must accept this judgment without question and react to it with equanimity. Any show of protest or of solidarity with the person so treated can be detrimental to one's career.

Within the contemporary workplace, familiarity and camaraderie are hollow. In a sincere relationship, friends are expected rise to each other's defense if there is an injustice and, at a minimum, to show compassion. Corporate culture discourages even this gesture, preferring to usher fired employees out of the building before other employees can become aware of the dismissal. Within an office environment, the individual is an abstract and meaningless object, standardized and dispensable, with no intrinsic value. They are "human resources" to be exploited or discarded. Corporations will claim to value their employees, even to the point of speaking of them as a "corporate family." But unlike a real family, a corporation will dispose of any employees that are seen as a burden or a threat to corporate goals.

Americans are particularly defenseless against this disingenuous, manipulative, exploitative scheme, which exploits the utilitarian streak in American culture. Psychologist Stanley Milgram, among others, suggests that Americans are far less likely than others to remain true to principles that conflict with rational calculations. They tend to automatically conclude that if an action is rational, then the principles that conflict with it must be invalid. Rather than rationally assess whether principles are being followed, they determine how to realign their principles with their rational interests. Rather than being a weapon in defense of principle, rationality becomes corrosive to it.

As Henry David Thoreau put it, "Men have become the tools of their tools." Many of us can see that our actions at work are causing damage. If we are not directly involved in the destruction or exploitation of life, we are aiding a machine that is. The resulting cognitive dissonance would normally be sufficient to cause many of us to quit our jobs, but the sad reality is that many of us prefer to rationalize away our conflicted value systems, lie to ourselves and suppress any thought that causes us psychological discomfort. Of those of us who dwell in an office environment, most are aware of this compromise and feel at least mildly conflicted by it. The rest are consummate robopaths; their robopathic education is complete.

7. Social Machines

We think of social groups as objects, unquestioningly accepting their existence as a fact. We think of the government as a real, solid thing—as permanent and eternal as the ground beneath our feet and the stars that stud the heavens above. But the government does not actually exist in any concrete sense, nor do corporations or militaries. Yes, we ascribe to them ownership of offices, real estate and other physical possessions, but a desk is not a government any more than you are your toaster. These are social inventions—fictions, to be exact. Their only physical presence is in the form of energy flows within our brains. They can be useful because they can help us organize the complexities of everyday life into recognizable patterns. And they can be harmful because they can motivate, condone and absolve us of murder, robbery, kidnapping and environmental destruction.

Social groups, be they clubs, towns, provinces, nation-states or international organizations, often start out as voluntary organizations. Your parent's bridge club didn't seek to enslave you or make you play for its profit. Social groups take on the characteristics of the people within them—for better or worse, but rarely does it turn out to be significantly worse—at least initially.

Some social groups exploit their members as though they were merely resources to be used up and discarded: cults, oppressive workplaces, despotic governments. They do not exist to serve their members, but rather make their members serve them. Sociologist and historian Lewis Mumford called these exploitative organizations "social machines," because of their inherently inhumane and robotic functioning.

The difference between a social machine and a social organization is in their radically different priorities. A social organization tends to emphasize balance with its surroundings, working in a give-and-take fashion for mutual benefit, using resources sustainably, and living in balance with the environment. Like good families, they aren't primarily organized around making their members bring in a lot of money or obeying all of the rules as precisely as possible and punishing those who don't. In a social organization, the needs of the members are paramount.

In a social machine it is just the opposite: individuals are tools to be used for some set purpose without much regard for their well-being. Social machines emphasize competition, not cooperation. They strive to dominate, subjugate. They seek privilege and advantage. Left to operate without any moderating influence, they create an environment—both physical and social—that is unsuitable for human life.

People often assign human traits to social machines, under the mistaken belief that people are in charge of them: "Goldman Sachs is greedy," or "The United States government is arrogant." They believe that since a CEO heads a corporation and a president heads a nation, these social machines will exhibit their traits. However, the truth is that people do not run large social machines; *the social machines run the people within them.*

If a government's economic policies are destructive, an optimist might think it possible to convince it to be less destructive, while a pessimist will assume that its policies are intentionally damaging. Both of these viewpoints may have merit.

But there is also a third possibility, which is often ignored: that the government social machine has grown so large and complex that individuals who operate it can no longer influence its actions. While humans may be persuaded, the machine's motives are nonhuman. A social machine seeks power, money, growth—all expressible in arithmetic terms—but it cannot seek things it cannot measure, such as happiness, justice or compassion. Only humans and human groups can act in compassionate ways.

It's common for bureaucracies to try to solve any problem with more bureaucracy. Similarly, social machines seek to become as large as possible so that they can more easily dominate the societies within which they operate. Greater size makes them more powerful, and also makes them more resistant to moderating human influence, which is needed to limit the damage they cause to people and the natural world. If a corporation becomes large enough, it comes to be seen as indispensable to the functioning of the economy or "too big to fail," and is granted virtual immunity from prosecution. This is a problem most recently seen in financial and automotive industries, but could probably extend to any number of other sectors of the economy: media corporations, weapons manufacturers, pharmaceutical companies, and other industrial giants. The tendency to spread like cancer and grow ever-larger is built into every social machine's design.

Yablonsky identifies three main ways in which humanistic groups, such as families or communities, differ from social machines. First, humanistic groups value people for their intrinsic worth, rather than for the profits they can deliver for the group. To gain a sense of self-worth within a caring context people tend to cooperate rather than compete. Instead of struggling to gain a personal advantage, they can just be themselves, open and honest. Their interactions are mutually supportive, caring and nurturing—in stark contrast to the cold professionalism and personal indifference of the office environment.

Second, people within humanistic groups can be far more spontaneous, creative, and carefree. There is little pressure to strictly adhere to rules, schedules, prescribed modes of behavior or (with the exception of certain religious sects) forms of dress. The rules that do exist tend to be easy to understand and are seen as fair and generally beneficial.

Finally, within humanistic groups people have the latitude to act compassionately toward one another even when this does not serve the group's overall goals. Health and happiness of the group's members, rather than the maximum productivity and growth—are the goals.

Not all of the world's governments have turned entirely machinelike and efficiency-oriented, and not all families and communities are supportive, creative and compassionate. Indeed, as Yablonsky notes, it is relatively common for families to develop scripted forms of communication—distant, superficial interactions designed to hide problems and avoid conflicts. Some people may even find that they have more freedom to be themselves at work than when they are walking on eggshells trying to keep the peace at home. The family itself can become a social machine if it sets strict standards of behavior above absolute honesty and devotion.

Within social machines, people are under constant pressure to obey. When an entire society feels pressured to surrender its moral autonomy, to obey the dictates of the machine, what happens is a kind of social death. Interactions take on a zombie-like quality. People go through the motions of living without spontaneity or purpose.

Within social machines, an individual's material success is directly tied to their ability to conform. Bertram Gross, a political science professor at City University in New York and author of *Friendly Fascism*, wrote that a person could achieve small amounts of autonomy within the constraints of the system, but that ultimately such autonomy is an illusion. Even people who achieve positions of power must continue to serve the system or they lose their status:

> With seniority, sweat, or manipulation, people can get a better cell. With good behavior, [servants] can move from the boredom of routinized work into a sunny prison courtyard where they may enjoy expense accounts, professional mobility and mutual back-scratching, and select their own forms of dehumanized and dehumanizing labor. While rewards are distributed in accordance with each one's power and service to the system, the illusion of meritocratic justice is provided by computerized rating systems that, by purporting to report on intelligence and effort, strongly suggest the stupidity and immorality of the weak...

> The average worker would be the Job of the future. Suffering from boredom, apathy, alienation, and the erosion of any earlier dreams of rising in the world, he is prepared to hibernate forever. He takes out his aggressions on others, particularly those beneath him. With harmless words, unlike Job of the Bible, he curses his gods, his family and the "powers that be." But, in action, he goes alone passively and accepts his fate.

Lured by the promise of material assets, the average American is enveloped within a social environment that is alienating, seemingly arbitrary, and completely unconcerned with social needs. The "big bribe," as Lewis Mumford puts it, "turns out to be little better than kidnapper's candy."

Corporate ideas and values have penetrated our society in a way as revolutionary as any organizational advancement since organized religion. Michael Lerner, a doctor of philosophy and clinical psychology, argues that humanistic groups have been largely displaced by their mechanical substitutes:

We might think of ourselves and of societies on a continuum. On the one end of the continuum, people approximate the extreme of caring only for themselves. On the other end, people begin to approach the biblical ideal: seeing every single human being as created in the image of God, and hence as infinitely precious and deserving of our caring and respect. On this end of the spectrum, we find people who concern themselves with improving the lot of immigrants and the homeless, for example, because they recognize these others as fundamentally connected to all of us.

Today, the family remains almost the only place where people can still be themselves, where life's dynamism and purpose are still preserved, where principled actions in defense of a loved one can still be expected and where we are not ultimately alone. If you are lucky enough to have a healthy, functioning family, you can expect it to make sacrifices for you.

Social machines have productive qualities that make them functionally superior to humanistic groups. When we are forced to weigh the pros and cons of allowing social machines to exist, the pros often win out. But if we are to retain our autonomy, our independent identities, if our lives are to have meaning beyond the blind pursuit of status and wealth, and if we are to avoid becoming alienated from one another, humanistic groups must be able to exert a decisive moderating influence on social machines.

> "Remember that I have power; you believe yourself miserable, but I can make you so wretched that the light of day will be hateful to you. You are my creator, but I am your master; obey!"
> —The monster to Victor Frankenstein, *Frankenstein*

8. Obey!

America's ruling institutions have a vested interest in controlling our behavior for the sake of efficiency. But just getting people to obey isn't enough for the efficiency-obsessed machines. To maximize efficiency, they need the total loyalty of their human moving parts. To this end, social control and propaganda is essential.

The most common method of control is through "framing." By using manipulatively phrased questions or commands, the machine can force people to act in a predictable manner. Leading questions, false equivalencies, "trigger" words such as "liberal," "Republican," "racist," encourage people to accept the frame and to ensure that they do not venture outside it. A politician who wants to advocate a policy of increased natural gas drilling might ask these two leading questions: "What should we do about the country's energy shortage?" and "How can we best exploit the nation's natural gas reserves?" Most people will automatically accept the premises that the nation has an energy shortage and that natural gas reserves should be exploited. The framing prevents critical examination of these premises, ignoring the natural gas glut (much of which is flared off) and the idea that it is best left in the ground (because atmospheric methane and CO_2 concentrations are already dangerously high).

Another way that authority figures can exact compliance is by offering a false choice. People will generally choose whatever they believe will be less painful or more pleasant. Refusing all together is not presented as an option. In this way, they unknowingly accept the framing placed upon them. Children who are just learning to manage their rational capacities are especially susceptible to this form of manipulation.

This sort of conditioning starts at a very young age. Dr. Sandra Crosser, a professor at Ohio Northern University and an author on issues of childhood development, writes that it is important for children, even toddlers, to be given choices and to *feel* as though they are in control of their lives. She writes:

"Would you like an apple or a banana?" Klaire's teacher asks. It is important to have a choice. It is especially important for Klaire to have a choice because Klaire is two. Why is it so important for a two-year-old to choose her snack? It is not particularly important whether Klaire chooses the apple or the banana. What is important is that she is given a real choice.

When a person is two [years old] there are many "you may nots." You may not: stay home alone, eat when you want, cross the street by yourself, lock the bathroom door, turn on the water, stay inside while the other children go outside, go to bed when you are ready, skip wearing boots, get yourself an aspirin, buy a guinea pig, or open the refrigerator. Because there are so many things a two year old may not be permitted to do simply because of safety or health precautions, it is difficult for two's to feel control in their lives. But this is exactly the time that a child needs to develop a sense of autonomy, a sense that he is an independent and competent individual in his own right.[62]

---

62 http://www.earlychildhoodnews.com/earlychildhood/article_view.aspx
?ArticleID=691

The presumption that children who are continually corralled, controlled and micromanaged may rebel is a correct one. But further coercing them into a narrow range of prescribed behavior by offering them false choices children are given a mere illusion of choice. One of the allowed answers to "Would you like an apple or a banana" must be "No." If it is not, then the child develops a fake sense of independence.

If it is possible to frame a decision by eliminating any possibility of a radical alternative, the social machine can ensure that the vast majority of its subjects will act within those constraints. All bureaucracies value predictability. If they can predict how people will react, they can control them much more easily, and this maximizes efficiency. And so they study people's reactions to certain stimuli, tally the results, then express them as mathematical formulas by which the likelihood of future actions can be calculated. Armed with this knowledge, social machines can more easily control the masses.

It's true that people have always been under pressure to obey the dictates of their culture and the wishes of their family and friends, but there is no comparing these with the pressures generated by our governing institutions. As Ellul observed, "there is no common denominator between the suppression of ration cards in an authoritarian state and the family pressure of two centuries ago. In the past, when an individual entered into conflict with society, he led a harsh and miserable life that required a vigor which either hardened or broke him. Today the concentration camp and death await him; [the bureaucracy] cannot tolerate aberrant activities."[63]

Corporations, government bureaucracies and other social machines strip people of their autonomy, but they do not take away people's free will altogether. They merely make its exercise very unpleasant. We often tell ourselves that we have no other choice but to do our jobs, which may involve committing various inhuman acts. Acting rationally, we choose the least

---

63 Jacques Ellul, *The Technological Society*, 1954, p. 140

painful option.

All of us, with the exception of those whose minds have been warped or destroyed through horrific abuse or torture, are morally responsible for the continued existence of the social machines that control us. As Jean Paul Sartre said, "We are alone with no excuses... man is condemned to be free. If I am mobilized in a war, this war is my war. It is in my image and I deserve it. I could always get out of it by suicide or by desertion. For lack of getting out of it, I have CHOSEN it." By failing to rebel, he concludes, "we have the war we deserve."

A healthy society allows people to behave virtuously or wickedly, and face the consequences of their actions. We are at our most human when we are able to act out of an honest sense of self. But when the exercise of free will is so cunningly thwarted, obedience becomes a sickness. If we accept Sartre's argument that "man makes himself" then our decision to obey is a decision to sell ourselves into slavery. A worker who allows himself to be enslaved voluntarily cultivates a personality that is compartmentalized, roboticized, and cowardly. If he is fully aware of the damage he is causing and yet continues to participate, then he corrupts himself. To quote James Baldwin, "People who shut their eyes to reality simply invite their own destruction, and anyone who insists on remaining in a state of innocence long after that innocence is dead turns himself into a monster."

9. Euphemisms

Totalitarian absolutism often goes hand in hand with a distorted language. Within a highly regimented society, there is a strong inclination—both in large institutions and in individuals—to control everything that can be controlled. This urge to control leads to excesses in the imposition of rules, in data collection and spying and in doling out punishments. To the bureaucratic mind, reality must be shaped, described and catalogued. Rule-makers often try to shape reality, to make it conform to their vision, by changing our shared vocabulary. This is most apparent in the phenomenon of political correctness, where certain words and expressions are effectively outlawed to ensure that no one is offended and to maximize the range of any political message. The growing awareness and sensitivity to "trigger" words is part of this trend. In academia and mass media, certain words have become too risqué to joke about or even to mention. This attitude toward the use of language and the tendency to self-censor has spread to social groups beyond the traditional political and commercial spaces. The reaction to certain words like the N-word, even when uttered in the most professional and sensitive context, is a taboo. People become visibly uncomfortable whenever it is uttered. The circumstances do not matter; the words themselves become fetishized and are more important than the intent behind them.

Industrialized societies have developed numerous terms to quantify and characterize efficiency, production, and violence. Social machines take this tendency to extremes, producing an impenetrable corporate-speak. What does it mean to be "leveraging" products into "vertical markets" or "powering a robust impact?" In its more extreme forms, corporate jargon is so loaded that it becomes a barrier to understanding, but this seems to be intentional. Only those already ensconced within the corporate power structure can fully make sense of this gibberish, ensuring that those on the outside are unable to understand—and therefore unable to criticize—what they are hearing or reading.

Cults use a similar method to establish a sense camaraderie and ésprit de corps among their members. By the use of jargon, the initiates are made to feel special, part of a holy mission of importance, for which they must make sacrifices. Once the jargon becomes part of one's internal narrative, it makes it difficult to communicate with outsiders in a direct manner, isolating the members from society.

Quasi-academic jargon creates the illusion of scientific precision and rationality in reaching decisions. The military bureaucracy has embraced the use of antiseptic euphemisms such as "collateral damage," which hides mass killings behind an innocuous-looking façade. The terms "operational exhaustion" or "Post-Traumatic Stress Disorder" are used to disguise the fact that many war veterans return as physical and emotional cripples. Peacetime becomes "the pre-war era," making war sound like the normal state of affairs whereas it is highly abnormal. Once the oblique terminology is firmly established, it becomes unprofessional to directly and clearly identify what is actually happening. The use of such euphemisms has become compulsory at high levels of the official establishment.

Within bureaucratic organizations, the most important air to exude is neither compassion nor brutality, but rather dispassionate, clinical competence. Euphemistic language helps to create emotional distance. As George Orwell wrote, "The whole tendency of modern prose is away from concreteness"— in this case, with the goal of avoiding having to face the full moral implications of an act.

When you accept a pseudo-scientific euphemism in place of a vernacular, down-to-earth term, you warp reality—not only for those you are addressing, but for yourself as well. "Ready-made phrases" as Orwell calls them, "construct your sentences for you—even think your thoughts for you, to a certain extent—and at need they will perform the important service of partially concealing your meaning even from yourself."[64]

George Orwell

The use of euphemisms is always a psychological control method, and an obvious one. But another, often ignored sub-category of psychological control is the pressure of euphemisms enshrined in written law. Here, euphemisms do not just distort the world views of individuals, but instruct entire bureaucracies. Military actions are carefully worded to neutralize potential legal challenges. Premeditated murder is sanitized by referring to it as "targeted killing." Even that is too strong; the stated intent isn't to kill, since that would be murder, but simply to "neutralize" an opponent. Acts of war are now called "kinetic military actions." The intent is not just to obscure the reality for critics in the media or within the government, but to preemptively redefine these actions in the event of a legal challenge, since many of them would be deemed illegal if they were identified for what they are. Only

---

64 George Orwell, *Politics and the English Language*

the Congress can declare war, but a mere administrative decision is all that is required to authorize a "kinetic military action."

Anthropologists are apt to say that culture finds its shape through language. Cities are often renamed by their conquers. Slaves are made to take the last names of their masters. Weapons of war, like the Apache helicopter, are named after conquered nations. It is notable that while numerous native tribes have named themselves after elements of the natural world, the technological man names natural phenomena after himself (e.g. Hurricane Sandy, Tropical Storm Bill, etc.) Change the language, and you change the culture.

Conversely, when certain words are eliminated from the public lexicon, it becomes difficult, if not impossible, to conceptualize what those words once represented. Orwell noted that totalitarian societies would alter the meanings of words to obliterate their presence in the world: "War is Peace, Freedom is Slavery, Ignorance is Strength." But a society need not be blatantly totalitarian to erase or alter the meanings or uses of words. It need only have a conscious or subconscious desire to do so.

In the Bible's creation story, God gives Adam the authority to name his creatures. While this is not stated directly, it is implied that this is where God first gave man the power to speak, since language had not been mentioned before. Genesis 2-19 reads: "Whatever the man called each living creature was then its name." Read it again more carefully. "Each living creature was then its name" means that the animals conformed to whatever verbal portraits Adam choose to paint of them. Thus, in the world's best-known creation story, words shaped reality, not the other way around. Later, in John 1-1, the Bible asserts that all creation sprouted from "the word." It reads: "In the beginning was the Word: the Word was with God and the Word was God." It was much the same with the classical pagans: the ancient Greeks agreed that words shape our values and our understanding of reality. Protagoras wrote: "The human being is the measure of all things: of things that are, that they are; and of things that are not, that they are not."[65] To Protagoras and his contemporaries, perception of reality emanated from each individual's ability to conceptualize it.

Some ancient Greeks, like the rhetorician Gorgias, went a step further. He saw the inflection of words as a kind of power equal to physical force and akin to godlike persuasion. Words carry what he called *dunamis*, literally translating to "potential" or "power." (In Latin, this word is rendered as "potentia.") In Gorgias' essay, "Encomium of Helen," he argues that words have as powerful an effect on the human experience as any drug:

> For just as different drugs draw off different humors from the body, and some put an end to disease and others to life, so too of discourses: some give pain, others delight, others terrify, others rouse the hearers to courage, and yet others by a certain vile persuasion drug and trick the soul.[66]

Despite the great power of words, they are, to Gorgias, inherently deceitful. Sometimes called the world's first nihilist, in his treatise, "On the Nonexistent" Gorgias argued that objective reality may not even exist, but even if it does and we can somehow sense reality, words may not fully communicate the substance of that reality.[67] Contemporary westerners believe that words are only a path to truth or falsehood, and that rhetoric is a vehicle or a tool that can be employed for good or evil. But to Gorgias's mind, truth could never really be achieved because rhetoric could be used to argue any proposition, even an absurd one. Since our senses are subjective, words are the basis by which we can define truth and the filter through which we see reality. Thus, those who control the lan-

---

65 Michael Grant, *The Classical Greeks*, p. 72
66 http://www.classicpersuasion.org/pw/gorgias/helendonovan.htm
67 http://users.wfu.edu/zulick/300/gorgias/negative.html

guage also control our reality.

Our daily experience bears eloquent testimony to this view. Our vision of reality is influenced by bureaucratic institutions which emphasize or exclude certain words. Imagine, what would a victim of a crime feel like if the word "victim" ceased to exist? A victim of a crime might feel an immense sadness and bitterness after being mistreated, but could not explain it succinctly—simply by saying, "I am a victim." But bureaucracies function in just this way: if they cannot quantify or commodify justice or morality in terms of productive, measurable outcomes, they cannot recognize it. Bureaucratic culture and those who dwell within it are entirely unable to perceive ethereal values of love, respect, and altruism. Those of us who are not fully immersed in the morass of bureaucracy can understand of the importance of these values and relate them through words. But this is becoming harder, as more and more people find their language displaced by the euphemisms of bureaucratic culture. Like native societies around the world who have seen their ancient languages and cultures displaced by the pidgins and creoles imposed by their colonizers, we are now seeing the last vestiges of human culture replaced by a mechanical, commercial, morality-free intelligence.

* * *

On the surface, most of American society seems deceptively nonviolent (except for the steady destruction wrought by the government or the occasional mass shooter.) Direct, personally motivated forms of physical violence are suppressed, especially among the educated, professional class, but linger in the form of repressed desire, because violence is a natural response to oppression. And so it manifests itself in cryptic, socially acceptable ways—when a school administrator harshly punishes a student for a minor transgression, or when a bureaucrat takes a perverse pleasure in making it illegal to feed the homeless. It is in such moments that the especially venomous nature of bureaucratic violence can be observed. The rule enforcer—simultaneously a mild-mannered professional and an aggressive, unsympathetic monster—is unable to act out repressed rage in any other socially acceptable way than by doling out punishments, fines, rejections, expulsions and other forms of objective, systemic violence.

The result is what Martin Luther King Jr. called a "negative peace." Our seemingly mild-mannered society is not in a state of true peace (because that would require justice) but is merely maintaining the illusion of peace. There is an undercurrent of intense rage bubbling just below the surface, looking for any socially acceptable outlet.

Sadism has becomes the only acceptable form of self-therapy for the American bureaucrat. The urge to punish with extreme prejudice has become commonplace. The punishments must be doled out indifferently and impassively, because passion is a threat to bureaucratic efficiency. Bureaucracies are forced to discard those who are obviously bloodthirsty. As political scientist Zygmunt Bauman writes, "passion sniffs evidence of its own failure."[68] The obviously passionate bureaucrat cannot help but disclose and accept responsibility for his actions; only the seemingly unemotional the indifferent bureaucrat can effectively avoid all blame. This is what it means to be civilized.

Can such a system be reformed? There is no possibility of reforming bureaucracy through reason, since reason is the bureaucrat's own *terra firma*. It offers us only false choices and hands all important decisions to bureaucrats. The only way to challenge such a system is by withholding all cooperation, even if unto death, as the early Christians challenged Rome. To motivate such a change would require a cultural revolution that changes the entire system of values. It's very difficult to imagine this because our culture is already so corrupt. What if

---

68 Zygmunt Bauman, *Modernity and the Holocaust*, p. 225

our language, suffused with euphemisms, can no longer express the thoughts such a revolution would require?

> "Step by step they were led to things which dispose to vice, the lounge, the bath, the elegant banquet. All this in their ignorance they called civilization, when it was but a part of their slavery."
> —Tacitus, *Agricola*

10. The Cultural Wasteland

Much has been written about the demise of American culture, from our constant demand for graphic displays of violence to the endless recycling of commercialized content. In place of culture we find industry—the entertainment industry, which specializes in delivering the perverse pleasures of form over substance, callous emotion over subtle beauty, instant gratification over the sometimes painful and disquieting pursuit of truth and beauty. What we call culture today is but a distant echo of the old myths and stories that have defined what it means to be human. Real culture forms reality, while the entertainment industry distracts from it. Not only is commercial culture fake but, worse yet, it functions as yet another form of social control: it reinforces crass consumerism and hyperindividualism—which are profitable for the money-making social machines and destructive of the communal values that can get in the way of maximizing productivity and profitability.

The bureaucratic mindset hasn't just deformed our work and family relationships, but also our creative drives. The entertainment industry is a waste management industry: it recycles video games and comic books into gritty film franchises, creating visions in which wonder, creativity and ideas of any value are notably absent. The irony is that this style of utilitarian realism in the commercial arts is even more of an illusion. The demand for "reality" in the arts, specifically in the call for gritty and realistic interpretations of childhood obsessions, is part of a trend toward abolishing all inconsistency in art. True art, which is filled with abstractions and unrealities, has been displaced by shallow renderings that leave nothing to the imagination. Behind the desire to extinguish real art and creativity lurks a fear that reality may at some point have to be addressed. Comic Book writer Alan Moore essentially agreed, saying in an interview with *The Guardian*, "It looks to me very much like a significant section of the public, having given up on attempting to understand the reality they are actually living in, have instead reasoned that they might at least be able to comprehend the sprawling, meaningless, but at-least-still-finite 'universes' presented by DC or Marvel Comics."[69]

Alan Moore

The entertainment industry may entertain, but it provides no answers or insights. The few messages that do manage to survive the process of art by committee are the ones that social machines feed on: violence works, growth is good, you can succeed and change the world if you believe in yourself and work hard. We may point to a few favorite exceptions as evidence that there is some value left in our mass media—Stanley Kubrick movies, or the TV series "Breaking Bad"—but if you are reading this, then *you* yourself

69 http://www.theguardian.com/books/2014/jan/21/superheroes-cultural-catastrophe-alan-moore-comics-watchmen

are an exception. (You are reading a book about bureaucracy and its effect on mental health. It's not exactly representative of most of the reading public's tastes!)

By commodifying our art, we have mechanized it. The culture itself has become a sort of social machine, directing people to serve its needs, rather than enlightening them, nurturing them, purifying their emotions and firing their imaginations.

It doesn't help that for most of us, culture controls our actions in ways that are largely invisible. In a sense, culture already functions like a machine. It resist the dictates or desires of individual entities, be they people, corporations or governments. No single person, whether a major celebrity or a head of state, can easily alter people's interests or tastes, how they interact with one another, their values and norms.

A substantive change in a culture usually requires either a catastrophic disaster (war, plague, economic collapse, etc.) or a revolutionary technological development like the invention of moveable type, television or the internet. Granted, an individual (Philo Farnsworth) created the technology for television, but his invention didn't become revolutionary in isolation, but only as part of a social trend. There have been numerous other inventions that claimed to change everything but actually changed nothing.

When someone attempts to singlehandedly alter the culture, with rare exception the outcome is either minimal change or no change at all. When during the 1980s and early 90s Nancy Reagan launched an anti-drug campaign titled "Just Say No", there was a conscious awareness of the effort among the general public, but there is no evidence to suggest that it was effective in actually reducing drug use. More successful public crusades targeting smoking and drunk driving took years and constant media pressure to have any effect.

In an entertainment-based culture, depth and meaning become discarded or undervalued, and the language itself takes on mechanical qualities. Subtleties—like metaphor and double-entendre—become harder to grasp. Metaphors invariably draw attention to the fact that much of our language, along with our reality, is formed through reinterpretation—something a rule-obsessed bureaucrat would be loath to admit. But the bureaucrats can rest easy: indifference to the subtleties of language is becoming quite widespread. We know that people diagnosed with Attention Deficit Hyperactivity Disorder (ADHD) and autism can have difficulty with the ambiguity of language, but teachers now complain that many apparently normal students are increasingly unable to understand metaphors.

Scientific studies support their observations. Kyung-Hee Kim, an educational psychologist at the College of William and Mary wrote a paper in 2011 describing what she called a "creativity crisis." She wrote that students have become "less emotionally expressive, less energetic, less talkative and verbally expressive, less humorous, less imaginative, less unconventional, less lively and passionate, less perceptive, less apt to connect seemingly irrelevant things, less synthesizing, and less likely to see things from a different angle." Even though IQ scores have been increasing, creativity scores have remained steady or decreased from sixth grade on. But the biggest decline is in "creative elaboration": the ability to expand upon an idea in a new way. Writing in *Psychology Today*, Dr. Peter Gray writes that Kim's findings show "more than 85 percent of children in 2008 scored lower on this measure than did the average child in 1984." He concludes: "For several decades we as a society have been suppressing children's freedom to ever-greater extents, and now we find that their creativity is declining."[70]

Without creativity, there can be no abstract thought, and ultimately no art. Art is always a rejection of reality-as-convention. The abstract and ambiguous nature of art is intolera-

---

70 https://www.psychologytoday.com/blog/freedom-learn/201209/children-s-freedom-has-declined-so-has-their-creativity

ble to the rule-beset mind that can only find meaning in consistency and order. Camus notes this in *The Rebel*, highlighting history's intolerance of art in times of political upheaval. During the French Revolution, no significant new poets emerged, and those that did were sent to the guillotine. The Protestant Reformation had religious forms of art all but abolished. Whenever we see art attacked by the state, it is because it sees art as a threat: the population it is struggling to control may use art to reinterpret reality. When the public ignores art, such a danger to the state no longer exists. Shortly thereafter, the culture can be pronounced dead.

Living in a dead culture

Theologian and social worker Stephen Jenkinson speaks and writes compellingly on the cheery subject of death. In the course of his social work at a hospital, Jenkinson has spent a lot of time around dying people and their families. He argues that in any sane culture dying is easily understood and embraced. There is sadness, but people do not try to escape it or avoid talking about it. The dying person doesn't try to push family away to spare them the discomfort of countenancing death. Dying is better understood, and there is less loneliness and bitterness for everyone involved.

Typically in America, quite the opposite happens. Most people are unlikely to see much death in their lives, even though it is as normal a part of human experience as life itself. Children are shielded from it. Many people try to hide or deny their terminal sickness. Many doctors stand firmly in the way of their patients accepting the inevitability of their death. When the family visits a dying grandparent, little is said that would draw attention to the obvious fact the grandparent is dying. The reflex is for everyone to retreat, both physically and emotionally.

A dying culture elicits similar reactions. People refuse to face it. Instead of dealing with its passing, cultural icons are endlessly recycled and redecorated, sequel after sequel, re-make after remake. Long-expired TV and film franchises are jolted back to life and placed back on life-support. Adolescence never ends, and the trappings of childhood are preserved long into adulthood, numbing the pain of a reality that, for many people, has no place for them. People struggle to rekindle the magic they once felt in their youth, trying to coax one more tortured breath out of what is now clearly dying. A kind of cultural necrophagia—the devouring of the dead—is now a dominant cultural trait. We need to move on; but what do we move on to?

In a recent interview, Jenkinson said:

> Because our way of life, on the surface, is so compellingly victorious, to think it's actually a calamity that just hasn't quite collapsed upon itself yet, it takes enormous sight to recognize. If your culture is endangered by our syndrome, it's very challenging not to opt for the syndrome as the solution.

> You might say you feel alienated? So what? It does nothing but contribute to the death spiral if you say, "I was never taught anything but how to feel alienated, so I'm going to remain so." It's much braver to say "I'm going to try my damnedest to be human."

> If you are willing to learn your dying culture, it will be very hard to be fearful and lonely as an older person. You will have some skill at being a human being and being human with other people. That's where it comes from. Not from things going great, or taking out an insurance policy so you don't get hurt. It comes from the hurting part.

Machines have no conscience

Freud pointed out that neurosis was the central emotional disorder of his time. It has certainly continued to be important in our time, along with psychopathy, psychosis and schizophrenia. Today Freud's central emotional disorder is so widespread that it is now regarded as normal to develop a kind of split personality—to compartmentalize one's work from one's personal life—even if this means living a double life. Many of us are sincerely nurturing toward a chosen few and utterly ruthless toward the rest.

Quoting philosopher-psychiatrist Dr. Erich Fromm, Aldous Huxley wrote in his essay "Brave New World Revisited":

> The real hopeless victims of mental illness are to be found among those who appear to be most normal. "Many of them are normal because they are so well adjusted to our mode of existence, because their human voice has been silenced so early in their lives that they do not even struggle or suffer or develop symptoms as the neurotic does." They are normal not in what may be called the absolute sense of the word; they are normal only in relation to a profoundly abnormal society. Their perfect adjustment to that abnormal society is a measure of their mental sickness. These millions of abnormally normal people, living without fuss in a society to which, if they were fully human beings, they ought not to be adjusted.

The highly regimented society is still relatively new to the human experience. For thousands of years, humans have enjoyed a communal culture that still allowed for individual autonomy. This remained true even in early industrial society, where a person could easily see and understand the benefits of working together. Today's machines, both physical and social, require complex, nonintuitive interactions; only blind faith in rules can fill the bureaucrats that animate them with any sort of meaning.

Today's Americans find themselves hemmed in by an organizational structure that confines their choices within extremely narrow parameters. The growth of bureaucratic power structures, coupled with the totalitarian possibilities of technology, suggests that we are heading toward a future with even less autonomy. As surveillance technology grows evermore invasive, it is reasonable to assume that the psychological pressure to both follow and enforce ever-more complicated rules will increase.

Science fiction authors often pit man against machine. In

Aldous Huxley

film and television, this conflict is often portrayed as overtly violent. *2001: A Space Odyssey*, *Terminator*, *Blade Runner*, *Westworld*, *The Matrix* all warn of the dangers of artificial intelligence turning on their creators. Sci-fi writers and futurists believe that in the near future humankind will create an artificial intelligence that will become smarter than it, and which then, for whatever reason, will decide to eradicate or control humankind by eliminating all human freedom. The boot that George Orwell imagined would stomp on a human face forever will be worn by a robot. What few people realize is that this robot has already been built, and has successfully enslaved increasingly large numbers of us. Bureaucracy has perverted just about every social interaction, invading even the most intimate spaces. It has made the teacher into an informant, ready to pounce on any failing, the peace officer into a soldier ready to shoot to kill without warning, and the spiritual guides, priests, reporters and other truth-tellers into propagandists, spies or unscrupulous public relations officers. Where before the ambitions of men might have endangered thousands, the bureaucratic social machine has enabled the enslavement, poisoning and murder of millions—perhaps even billions—not yet born.

As individuals, we are nearly powerless to cause any meaningful change in the social machine's direction or goals. Only a few people at the top of the hierarchy have any power to effect any sort of change, and even they, whether they realize it or not, must function within the strict confines of the system. The futility of it all produces an all-pervading feeling of meaninglessness, magnified by the understanding that we are all replaceable—and will be replaced should we try to exercise our autonomy.

Freud theorized that the superego—which is basically our conscience—causes a person act in a socially acceptable manner. It works in opposition to the id, which is a person's instinctive drive. A person's superego is developed during the early stages of life and is influenced primarily by parents, but also by teachers and by other people that act as role models. In a healthy society, the superego encourages compassion, patience and respect. In a society of robopaths, values of conformity and obedience dominate the superego, allowing its members to engage in morally reprehensible acts with minimal psychological discomfort.

In *Civilization and Its Discontents*, Freud notes that the culture's broader values, what he called the cultural superego, have an enormous effect on shaping each individual's superego. In other words, society's cultural values—its moral compass—influences all the people collectively. John Ralston Saul calls it the "Unconscious Civilization," in which technology, despite the large amount of freely available knowledge, has only made us less aware of ourselves. Marxists refer to this overarching influence as the superstructure. Sociologist Lewis

Mumford called it the Megamachine. Jacques Lacan described the symbolic order between individuals as the "big Other." Regardless of which name one uses, and which specific attributes one assigns to it, there is a consensus that outside of an individual's mind there exists a system of influences which compete and complement one another. The culture itself is a social machine—the biggest one of all—and it determines the rules by which all other social machines operate. In the United States, the rules or moral imperatives which dominate us and which set the standards of behavior include conformity, obedience, psychological comfort, efficiency and speed—and all of these are beneficial to production but harmful to humanistic values. Critics of corporations like to point to their psychopathic nature as the source of our social and economic problems, but they often fail to see that capitalism can only thrive in a psychopathic culture.

As our culture has been hijacked by social machines, it has had a frightening effect on our psychology. Social historian Yuval Noah Harari recently noted that our culture is moving away from the conscious human being toward something totally rational and hyper-intelligent—and unconscious:

> Throughout history, intelligence always went hand in hand with consciousness... We are developing non-conscious algorithms that can play chess, drive vehicles, fight wars and diagnose diseases better than us. When the economy has to choose between intelligence and consciousness, the economy will choose intelligence. It has no real need for consciousness... Within a century or two, Homo sapiens will disappear and will be replaced by completely different kinds of beings. Beings more different from us than we are different from Neanderthals.[71]

71https://www.adbusters.org/magazine/121/aware.html

If Harari turns out to be correct, then the next stage in human evolution will not be defined by our merging with technology—which has already happened—but rather by our surrender of consciousness. In the interim, there is evidence to suggest that our toys, electronics, and work devices have already caused us to begin that transition.

Beset by gadgets

There is certainly no shortage of writing on the topic of "techno-buffoons" and what writers like Derrick Jensen call "electronic hallucinations," but their near-universal acceptance within American culture demands that we briefly summarize their effects. High technology has successfully penetrated all income levels and social classes. It has reshaped how we interact with each other and the world. The hollowing-out of community life may have started with the automobile and television, but the funneling of virtually all social activity into computers and smartphones is reshaping human interaction to an extent never before thought possible. According to Pew Research, 98 percent of Americans between the ages of 18 and 29 own a cell phone, and of these an unknown number is hopelessly addicted to them.[72] Even the homeless in America have access to cell phones. In some areas, governments subsidize their cost, because they are now seen as an indispensable tool for finding a job. "Necessity," John Milton wrote, is "the tyrant's plea."

The widespread movement to get laptops or handheld tablets into the hands of every schoolchild, rich or poor, is seen as a worthy goal. In the UK, in 2010 Prime Minister Gordon Brown announced a plan to get a laptop for every schoolchild in the country: "We want every family to become a broadband family, and we want every home linked to a school... The nationwide roll-out of our home access program to get laptops and broadband at home for 270,000 families...

72http://www.pewinternet.org/fact-sheets/mobile-technology-fact-sheet/

will mean all families can come together, learn together and reap rewards together."[73] Brown also promised that all schools will have online reporting, to allow parents to monitor their child's progress. Programs such as One Laptop, One Child propose to do the same for students in developing countries. But the promise of computers to deliver improved academic performance is entirely unproven. Many critics say that computers only add another distraction to the learning process. Students with access to computers will certainly learn to use them—and neglect to learn other essential skills. At an annual meeting of the Association of Teachers and Lecturers (ATL), a teachers union in the United Kingdom, teachers reported on students who had an impressive ability to interact with computers, but lacked the ability to focus, or to manipulate physical objects in a real-world environment.

In an article on "iPad addiction," the UK's telegraph quotes Colin Kinney, a teacher from Northern Ireland, who said that his colleagues would "talk of pupils who come into their classrooms after spending most of the previous night playing computer games and whose attention span is so limited that they may as well not be there." Electronic connectivity has displaced the natural, human way of connecting.

> I have spoken to a number of nursery teachers who have concerns over the increasing numbers of young pupils who can swipe a screen but have little or no manipulative skills to play with building blocks or the like," said Kinney. Pupils who are obviously unable to socialize are accompanied by parents who "talk proudly of their [child's] ability to use a tablet or smartphone.

Dr. Richard Graham, a psychiatrist and psychotherapist who treats adolescents at Capio Nightingale Hospital in London, made national headlines in 2013 when he noted that indi-

---

73 http://www.telegraph.co.uk/education/6963502/Free-laptops-and-broadband-to-help-poor-families.html

viduals addicted to technology showed symptoms similar to alcoholics or heroin addicts when going through withdrawal. "Children have access to the internet almost from birth now," he said. "They can't cope and become addicted, reacting with tantrums and uncontrollable behavior when [the gadgets are] taken away. Then as they grow older, the problem only gets worse." The hospital offers a 28-day "digital detox" program which can cost up to $26,000 to help parents unable to ween their children off technology.

John Ralston Saul

The source of young people's inability to socialize can be traced to what happens to them quite early in life. A recent study by Princeton University reported that "40 percent of infants in the U.S. live in fear or distrust of their parents, and that will translate into aggressiveness, defiance and hyperactivity as they grow into adults. Of that number, 25 percent don't bond with their parents because the parents aren't responding to their needs. And a tragic 15 percent find their parents so distressing that they will avoid them whenever possible."[74]

As these children mature, they can be expected to have increased difficulty relating to others, and lack the understanding that needed for empathy and compassion. At an intellectual level, these children are still like infants. It's entirely appropriate that the word "infant" comes from the Latin *īnfāns*, meaning unable to speak, because it is conceivable that the up-

---

74http://abcnews.go.com/Technology/love-means/story?id=23208782

coming generation may be unable (not just unwilling) to communicate adequately. Technology may compensate for the inability to communicate in person, but not for the inability to empathize. So far, technology has utterly failed to bring people closer together and reduce their isolation—quite the opposite.

Essayist John Ralston Saul points out that while schools try to sell the idea of providing every student with a computer as a way of providing them with an entry point to a wonderful world of knowledge and understanding, what they are really aiming for is a way to standardize a thoughtless form of learning:

> Once in possession of enough equipment they can line up a classroom full of students behind machines where they can be educated in isolation by something less intelligent than a human. This sacrifices one of the primary purposes of education...—to show individuals how they can function together in society.[75]

Excessive solitude caused by being trapped in front of a gadget afflict both the young and the old. A study by AARP indicated that roughly 35 percent of Americans 45 years old or older were lonely.[76] In a world of effortless yet superficial social interaction mediated by computerized devices, people are feeling more isolated than ever.

One of the counterarguments often heard when someone criticizes digital technology is the insistence that technology helps to reinforce social bonds that might otherwise atrophy. For several generations now the telephone has helped to support and maintain relationships that would otherwise wither due to physical distance. And now the internet serves a similar function, reuniting friends and families who might otherwise

---

75 John Ralston Saul, *The Unconscious Civilization*, p. 139
76 http://www.aarp.org/personal-growth/transitions/info-09-2010/loneliness_2010.html

be forced to talk on the telephone, or (gasp!) pick up a pen and write a letter. But talking the phone or exchanging letters just isn't the same as meeting someone face to face. We are social animals, and the antidote to loneliness is intimacy, which distance makes impossible no matter how many gadgets are brought to bear.

The rate at which technology has displaced direct social interaction is stunning. To many people, a person without a smartphone, which is less than a decade old, might as well be living without electricity or indoor plumbing. The vast majority of people consider smartphones to be not just necessary, but beneficial. But what benefit is there in increased isolation and low quality relationships filtered through glowing screens? An article in *Slate* titled "Loneliness is Deadly" noted that isolation, whether self-imposed or not, directly contributes to health complications, responsible for more early deaths than obesity. Citing a study by AARP, the article notes that loneliness among adults has doubled from 20 percent in 1980 to 40 percent today. Worse, it goes on to say, loneliness directly contributes to the kinds of selfish and individualistic behavior we're seeing in America's bureaucracies:

> When we are lonely, we lose impulse control and engage in what scientists call "social evasion." We become less concerned with interactions and more concerned with self-preservation... Evolutionary psychologists speculate that loneliness triggers our basic fight vs. flight survival mechanisms, and we stick to the periphery, away from people we do not know if we can trust.

Like many articles about technology-induced social problems, it ends with an erroneous proposal which everyone knows won't work. In this sadly predictable case, the author suggests that internet dating could be a source of new relationships, even while the internet more generally contributes to the problem in other ways:

Couples who found each other online and stayed together shared more of a connection and were less likely to divorce than couples who met offline. If these statistics hold up, it would stand to reason friendships could also be found in this way, easing those whose instincts tell them to stay on the periphery back into the world with common bonds forged over the Internet.[77]

The solutions offered even by those who bemoan the widespread loneliness of gadget-riddled, internet-addicted life is essentially more of the same, because to suggest any kind of radical reversal would be so futile that it would be an admission of failure, leading to even greater despair. Yet actual solutions are not just conceivable—they are dead simple, and as close as the off-switch and the nearest electronics recycling center. By studying relatively technology-free lifestyles— such as those of people just one or two generations ago—we can learn a great deal about our own failings and look for ways to undo the damage.

77 http://www.slate.com/articles/health_and_science/medical_examiner/ 2013/08/dangers_of_loneliness_social_isolation_is_deadlier_than_obesity. html?wpsrc=fol_tw

"Power is not alluring to pure minds."
—Thomas Jefferson

"I want to be made out of protoplasm and last forever so Pat will love me. But fate has made me a machine. That is the only problem I cannot solve. That is the only problem I want to solve."
—Kurt Vonnegut, *EPICAC*

11. Bureaucracy and its Discontents

When I first began researching the disciplinary systems of American schools, I was confused and appalled. How could our nation's educators, whose goals are to support and nurture the development of young people, display such wanton disregard for the obvious negative consequences of their actions? But on some level, which was at first mostly subconscious, I did understand them: I too felt the pressure to conform to written rules for the benefit of bureaucratic neatness, to put things and people "in their proper place" and to align my actions with rules.

Trying to discover the origin of this pressure, I studied news reports and tried to follow the stories to their resolutions, hoping that someone would be able to explain the source of the numerous "unfortunate oversights.". But answers were elusive; at best, parents and students would decry the policies or the poor judgment of teachers and school administrators, but rarely would they go farther and ask why the policies were being enforced with such crass disregard for the circumstances.

Some suggested that teachers and school administrators were in fear of their jobs or of civil liability if some minor transgression they ignored were to lead to a violent incident. Fear may have explained some instances, but that explanation was ultimately unsatisfying. It also did little to explain why administrators would decide to dole out punishments without regard for the specific circumstances of each incident.

As I began to look into bureaucratic conduct more broadly, I began to see other examples of officials who enthusiastically, and in some cases gleefully, strove to make others conform to rules in hurtful ways. Anyone who has worked in retail long enough should be familiar with employees who take their low-paying, low-skill job very seriously. They insist on rejecting returns without a receipt or refuse to accept a coupon that is one day expired. You might think that people working repetitious, boring, low-paying jobs would relish the opportunity to ignore the rules, but the opposite is often true. Since they cannot break their chains, they instead find meaning in rattling them.

The cold and ruthless actions of bureaucrats are rooted in weak sense of personal identity. In a controlling and despotic society, positive social roles are rare and one's sense of self becomes illusory and elusive. The bureaucrat's inner life becomes unhitched from their professional and happy public image. The result is a sort of lunacy, or what mental health professionals might call "radical estrangement" or "hyperalienation." These are common symptoms of schizophrenia, literally meaning "split mind." Unlike many schizophrenics however, these psychologically damaged bureaucrats are quite good at blending in and obeying social norms. Their inability to act compassionately is always hidden behind the rules they worship.

Once you understand the source of the bureaucrat's simmering rage, it's hard not to feel sympathy for them. They are sad, lost people. Their lives are an endless quest for meaning. Whether life has meaning is one of the most paralyzing questions you can ask yourself. The need to do so usually arises in a crisis, prompted by a sudden awareness that your life may not have any meaning. Acting on this insight takes emotional and sometimes financial support, both of which are sparse in the United States today.

So what is the solution? Now that we understand the depth of this problem, how can we promote a society that values compassion, community, and other qualities which are needed to stave off bureaucratic insanity? First, we must acquiesce to what will not work and understand why past attempts to limit the growth of bureaucracy have failed. Only then will we be able to properly assess what methods might best reign in this raging beast.

The naïve and the delusional

Freud saw civilization itself as the root cause of the widespread neurosis he was witnessing. A neurotic may suffer from phobias, obsessive-compulsive disorders and generalized anxiety. Victims of these and many other psychological problems have always struggled to balance the conflicting demands of their psyche with those of the surrounding culture. In the past, America's collective madness has been pegged to prudish Puritan values, but today our alienated state originates from technophilia—a love of technology, efficiency and gadgets. Our technology fetish is a symptom, but not the true source of our problems. Its root causes are a culture of overbearing domination and a compulsion to create efficient hierarchical organizations that suppress individual autonomy.

Few have accurately diagnosed our society's problems; fewer still have proposed realistic solutions. We are bombarded from every direction with endless false hopes to satisfy our emotional needs. Hope takes on a number of different shapes: "Education, that's the way to achieve security! Then we'll be free to do what we want!" Or "Technology will save us!" Or the ever-popular "We just need a new president, one who truly feels our pain and isn't just a smooth talker. Then things will change!" Amazingly, many people fall for these false hopes repeatedly.

Critics from outside of the mainstream establishment often suffer from delusional and desperately hopeful thinking. The political left is especially entrenched in their naïveté; they await their revolution—a historic moment when people across the country and the world will suddenly realize that they are human, connected with one another, and responsible for one another—and when the revolution fails to arrive, they wait some more. They seem to believe that at some point the situation will become so toxic that people will finally be willing to set aside their short-term interests and get down to building some kind of new society. They will occasionally ask, "What is wrong with people?" but they never have an answer. They are unable to see society for what it is: an efficient control mechanism with very little allowance for autonomous action. They cannot see the real chains, on themselves or others. As Goethe wrote, "None are more hopelessly enslaved than those who falsely believe they are free."

There is little or no hope through electoral politics. Politicians for the most part do not appeal to our reasoning, but rather to our emotional need for meaning and purpose. National politics is always a tribal activity. We vote, then hope that, against all previous evidence, our elected officials will follow through on some of their promises. Our belief in hope is near sacrosanct. We tell ourselves, "We can never give up hope!" Hope is optimism but, as Oswald Spengler once said, "Optimism is cowardice."

Political activists often hope that we can implement structural reforms, such as the removal of money from politics. In recent years, presidential candidates like Salt Lake City mayor Rocky Anderson, Louisiana Governor Buddy Roemer and Harvard Law Professor Lawrence Lessig have run on platforms that promise to reign in big money in politics. There are numerous problems with this plan. First, it would require the government to limit itself in defiance of its design, which is to always try to expand its power to better serve the rich and the powerful. It would take a massive grass roots effort, which is unlikely for an electorate that is primarily concerned with identity politics and preserving their lifestyle options.

Let's not forget the indoctrinating power of the media. As the printing press created uniformity in language, it also created a uniformity of thought. Electronic communication, which indoctrinates even more efficiently, creates even greater conformity. Even with the relatively independent and free internet, the majority of the mass media narratives are shaped by corporations. Since the culture's control mechanisms are reinforced by media conglomerates, they would probably have to be shut down before an alternative system could gain traction. This isn't going to happen.

Even if we assume that the necessary changes are possible, there is an overarching system of control—a cultural imperative which ensures that rebels who manage to alter the direction of the media, the government or other institutions have limited impact. When one social machine is made to rebel against the culture's larger values—namely, efficiency—the other social machines, in a spontaneous burst of efficiency, rush in to put down the rebellion or limit its influence. The media engages in campaigns of distraction or denigration, or the government ensnares protesters in red tape or arrests the opposition leaders on spurious charges. That such abuses do happen should be obvious, but what's notable is that they always happen in support of the system's larger goals, namely to preserve and promote profitability and growth. Since this is a structural problem, it requires a structural solution—a culture-wide remaking of values, which hardly seems possible for us as individuals to even dream about. The various mechanisms within society support one another; a mesh of mutually supportive social machines makes it highly resistant to change.

Max Weber noted that "When those subject to bureaucratic control seek to escape the influence of existing bureaucratic apparatus, this is normally possible only by creating an organization of their own which is equally subject to the process of bureaucratization." An effective public protest must be well organized and, to some degree, hierarchical. A movement capable of dismantling the entire bureaucratic machine would need to use force in similar ways. If violence is used to defeat this civilizational paradigm, what would replace it? The new civilization might be different in name and symbolism, but not in its basic function. Without a thoroughly different culture, the replacement system would still be about profits and growth at any cost. Its claim of moral superiority would rest on the flimsy justification that it can destroy the natural world and subjugate the human race more equitably!

In short, positive large scale changes to the culture are hard to imagine and virtually impossible for any one person to implement. I am not going to bore you with a detailed policy discussion on ways to reform the nation's political system or its culture—because that is what every other book of this kind attempts to do—and fails. Most of those proposals are never implemented—because they cannot be implemented. Critics of the system are often blind to the extent to which human control of it has been marginalized. Those who do see the big picture admit there may be no stopping this trend short of some kind of catastrophe, which, most of them concede, is hardly desirable. Therefore, instead of concentrating on society-wide changes, let us concentrate on the minutia of everyday life, because that is the only place where you, as an individual, can still make a meaningful difference.

Practical resistance

Even though the bureaucratic system might be self-destructive, this thought provides little comfort for those of us forced to interact with it on a daily basis. Still, there are practical ways to insulate yourself and your family from the most egregious and controlling aspects of bureaucracy. The most obvious way is to wall yourself off from this inhuman system and watch it warily from a safe distance. The more distance you put between yourself and the system, both physically and emotionally, the less likely you are to be vulnerable to the unpredictable downside of our complex bureaucratic society. To this end, I want to discuss a few areas where the dangers are most prominent. Some of this may seem obvious, but it's worth examining just how bad things can get.

The police state

In general, large bureaucracies should be avoided as much as possible, because you can never tell when you will become the target of overzealous functionaries intent on making your life reflect their own inner devastation. Rarely is this truer than when dealing with the police. It would be unfair to say that most police are out to cause you misery for no reason, but they could, and that is reason enough to avoid them whenever possible.

Even if you do not believe yourself to be a typical target of police malfeasance, there is still a danger. Simply drawing the gaze of the police state can cause it to descend upon you quickly and without warning. Not a week goes by where I do not read about someone who innocently trusts the authorities —and is abused by them.

When I was a freelance journalist, I profiled a man who was held for 8 months on a rape charge. His accuser turned out to be an escaped mental patient. We located documents proving that she had escaped from an institution in Maryland and had hitchhiked north to Philadelphia, which is where she made the false accusation of rape. A query into this woman's past would have revealed her untrustworthiness, but despite serious inconsistencies and oddities in her story, the city attempted to prosecute the man anyway. In the end, the judge had to release the accused man because the city's attorneys could not produce the alleged victim, who had run off to another state. Even though the witnesses were unconvincing and the evidence circumstantial, the man was still held for the better part of a year before the judge dismissed the case. The point is, even the innocent can find themselves victimized by robotic, unreflectively tenacious government officials.

If the police search your home for evidence of a crime for which you would ultimately be exonerated, what are the chances that they might find something else to charge you with? They are not as small as you might think. Perhaps you own a gun with a few high capacity magazines—perfectly legal in some states, but in others construed as evidence of intent to commit a criminal act or an act of terrorism. Sometimes all it takes to commit a felony is to cross a state border: in New York State, possession of a magazine that can carry 11 rounds of ammunition or more is a class D felony, and carries a punishment equal to that for rape in the second degree or sexual abuse in the first degree.[78,79] That someone could be punished in this way isn't a theory. In 2013, Army veteran Staff Sgt. Nathan Haddad was charged with seven felony counts for possession of five 30-round magazines, illegal in New York State.[80] Haddad reached a plea deal and pleaded guilty to a lesser misdemeanor charger in exchange for probation, but had he been convicted of the original charge, he could have served up to seven years in prison.[81]

Even if you are convinced that you have nothing to hide, your bank statements, credit card bills, bottles of alcohol or drugs, and all the emails yo have ever sent or received could

---

78 http://ypdcrime.com/penal.law/article265.htm#p265.02
79 http://ypdcrime.com/penallawlist.php?
tfm_order=DESC&tfm_orderby=class
80 http://www.washingtontimes.com/blog/guns/2013/feb/6/miller-vet-arrested-high-capacity-magazines-new-yo/
81 http://www.watertowndailytimes.com/article/20130406/NEWS07/7040
69911

be used to create the illusion of a life in shambles and concoct a possible motive for a crime. Excess cash—which is anything over $500—could be used as evidence that you planned to flee or were engaging in illegal activities.

Asset forfeiture laws, currently unchallenged by most courts, allow local police to seize cash and other assets without a trial. The Washington Post reported that in 2014 police seized more assets by way of asset forfeiture than burglars, and grew at an average rate of 19.4 percent a year over the last 20 years.[82, 83]

If you ever find yourself at the mercy of this system, at best you will be forced to wage battle against a set of massive, unresponsive bureaucracies. Your private life could be exposed to the media or publicized on the internet. This could make it difficult or impossible to get a good job, since almost all employers will run an internet search on your name when you apply. At worst, you could be sent to prison for decades, or even for life.

You should always assume that the police are always ready to make an example out of you. When they approach you, treat them politely, but decline to provide any information beyond what they can demand of you by law. They may briefly detain you, but giving them the absolute minimum of data to act on will minimize the likelihood that they will arrest you or confiscate your belongings. Always keep in mind that the police are under no obligation to be truthful to you. While you may be compelled to speak up to defend your rights and dignity, no robopath is going to appreciate an impassioned speech on the importance of liberty and freedom. It is far more likely that the police would feel an impulse to bring you around to their way of thinking through brute force. Further, you should not

82 https://www.washingtonpost.com/news/wonk/wp/2015/11/23/cops-took-more-stuff-from-people-than-burglars-did-last-year/

83 https://www.armstrongeconomics.com/international-news/north_america/americas-current-economy/police-civil-asset-forfeitures-exceed-all-burglaries-in-2014/

presume that the police will follow, or even know, the law. The decision whether or not to arrest you is largely a matter of their individual discretion. Therefore, the best way to deal with the state's frontline foot soldiers is disengage from them as quickly as possible.

If you manage to avoid the state—say, by living in a low-crime, low-population area—you can still be dragged through the legal bureaucracy by frivolous lawsuits or by debt collectors, which will sap your funds even under ideal circumstances. To further insulate yourself, consider studying some of the various books which describe various methods for minimizing your exposure to government or private entities. The methods include implementing biometric security devices like fingerprint or retina scanners and encrypting the hard drives in their computers. They also point out the importance of securing photos and other private information from leaking out on the internet. Some go as far as to suggest even creating secret rooms to store sensitive items. Finally, for those truly concerned about being hounded by the state, debt collectors or private investigators, they provide readers with details on how to leave the country.

For these and other suggestions, I suggest the 3rd edition of J. J. Luna's *How to be Invisible.* For a more extreme and permanent escape from your current life, take a look at Frank M. Ahearn's *How to Disappear,* which provides methods to escape more serious threats and to lead your pursuers on a wild goose chase that ends in a cold trail,

Alternatives for education and job training

Both students and teachers are fleeing America's public schools, preferring instead to pursue private, and far less regulated, systems of education. For children and their parents, an increasingly popular way to escape the madness of our micromanaged public schools is through homeschooling. Over the last decade, the number of homeschoolers in the US has roughly doubled, and now stands at 1.5 million. While at present most homeschoolers are Anglo, other ethnic groups are beginning to homeschool in greater numbers. State legislatures have continually sought to regulate homeschooling, sometimes going as far as to require certifications for parents, but thus far the controlling urges of the state have been successfully countered by pro-homeschooling activists.

Despite anti-homeschooling myths—that homeschoolers are overly religious, or that homeschooled kids are badly socialized or unprepared for college—a survey by the National Household Education Surveys Program in 2009 found that "91 percent of homeschooled students had parents who said that a concern about the environment of other schools was an important reason."[84] Only 36 percent of homeschooled students were motivated primarily for religious reasons.[85] Parents who opt to homeschool their children tend to have a number of advantages over the other parents: they tend to be better educated, have higher levels of income, and often have two-parent households with only one working parent.[86]

Melissa Roy, a mother and blogger on homeschooling issues, admits that her motives are complicated. She cited "flexibility... the schedule... a lack of trust in the system, lack of agreement with policies and norms, lack of confidence in the education our children would receive and the type of environment they would spend so much time in." Some teachers feel threatened by the homeschooling movement, seeing it as an attack on their status in society, but Roy insists that she has nothing but admiration for professional educators: "Just because I chose a different path for my children, doesn't mean you are valueless... I can only hope that someday... teachers

84 https://nces.ed.gov/fastfacts/display.asp?id=91
85 https://nces.ed.gov/pubsearch/pubsinfo.asp?pubid=2009081
86 http://nces.ed.gov/pubs2003/schoolchoice/

can once again focus on just the students."[87]

Students are not the only ones trying to escape from the education system. Teachers are abandoning the profession in favor of work in private schools or give up teaching altogether and take office jobs. I know teachers who've left the profession to take jobs composing marketing posts for social media, taking phone calls for customer service and other entry-level jobs. When I asked one of them if she would ever consider returning to teaching, she said that she'd rather work at a low-paying, menial job. She compared teaching to slave labor: "The teaching day never ends. There's always something more to prepare or something to grade. For that kind of work, the pay is awful. And all the rules? The administration is completely unsympathetic."

I worked in educational software for seven years, and during this time we brought in dozens of current and former teachers for interviews. Only a few were willing to bash their employers during an interview, but a little prodding almost always revealed their resentment of the school's controlling and manipulative management. Some of these people were willing to put up with an hour-long commute for unrewarding work just to leave the public school system. Even as they tried to reassure us that they weren't desperate, their desire to escape was reflected in their mannerisms and colored their every interaction.

The situation in America's colleges is even worse. Powered by limitless loans backed by government guarantees, these once affordable institutions have turned into gateways to debt servitude and bankruptcy. Today there is more student loan debt than credit card debt.[88] Delinquency rates hover around 11 percent—nearly double the rate of just a decade ago.[89] Economists tend to say that going to college is still a good invest-

---

87 http://www.huffingtonpost.com/melissa-roy/teachers-this-is-not-abou_b_8125166.html
88 http://www.forbes.com/sites/halahtouryalai/2014/02/21/1-trillion-student-loan-problem-keeps-getting-worse/#4e42035516d3

ment despite the cost because jobs that require college degrees pay more. But how does something that you cannot sell, but rises in price faster than the income it generates, qualify as a "good investment?" And what is the overall return on investment if over half of the graduates cannot find jobs that are in any way related to their degree?

The failure to repay student loan debt is a serious, potentially criminal matter. Currently, it is impossible to discharge a student loan in bankruptcy. If a borrower defaults, this can even result in imprisonment. In Texas, the US Marshal Service has served between 1,200 and 1,500 warrants to those who had failed to repay their student loans.[90] I personally know many people who have had difficulties in repaying their student loans—which sometimes exceed $20,000, and, in one case, $100,000. This wasn't entirely their fault: most of them took on this debt before they were even out of their teens. Their decision to encumber themselves with what is essentially a mortgage-sized debt was influenced in part by their misunderstanding of the true state of the US job market, and in part by their general immaturity.

The obvious solution to the problem of onerous student debt is, of course, to refuse to take out such outrageous loans. There are low-priced alternatives: many local community colleges are relatively inexpensive and offer two-year programs that cover many of the liberal arts classes necessary for a four-year degree. It is conceivable that students could hold a part-time or even a full-time job during this time and be able to pay for the classes out of pocket. When they are ready to transfer to the and more expensive university, they can perhaps take out some loans, but continue to work, to save and to keep the debts from from piling up. Simply, by attending a community college first, students could reduce their student loan burden

89 http://www.washingtonexaminer.com/heres-why-student-loan-delinquencies-are-so-high/article/2570512
90 http://www.fox26houston.com/news/local-news/92232732-story

by as much as half. Admittedly, this approach doesn't eliminate educational debt altogether, and it won't stop the overall cartel-like behavior of America's higher education system, but it will help students avoid becoming financially handicapped by it before they are even 20 years old.

Alternatively, young people should seriously consider avoiding higher education altogether, by learning a trade. They can either accept an entry level job which provides on-the-job training, or attend a trade school, and become an electrician, a plumber, or an IT professional. The tyranny of college prep classes has made trade jobs appear inferior, but there is every reason to think that jobs which require college degrees will continue to become increasingly scarce, even without a serious economic calamity. On the other hand, trade jobs are difficult to outsource, are practical enough for personal use, and best of all, are relatively insulated from the bureaucratic machinations and regulatory overreach that has become so common in corporate office life. It seems inevitable that our society will eventually be forced to find new appreciation for trade jobs as more and more jobs that require college degrees are globalized away. It makes sense to stay ahead of the curve by developing a skill set that will remain in demand.

Many people choose to settle for lower-paying jobs for the sake of having only marginally greater autonomy. But if you want to permanently escape the micromanaging nature of bureaucratic institutions, you have to work for yourself. It is a route that has become increasingly difficult in most forms of commerce, where person-to-person interaction is minimized in favor of expensive and high-tech forms of order-taking, stock-keeping, shipping and maintenance. But working for yourself remains a viable option in the trades, such as plumbing, locksmiths, electricians, and other on-site supporters of infrastructure. For these indispensable and largely autonomous individuals, it is possible to develop a career that works *with* other people instead of working *for* manipulative social machines.

There are numerous other benefits to being self-employed. You can largely control the variables that impede your work. You can set your own schedule, to avoid traffic jams, or even to work from home as often as you like. Unlike an office job, where your routine is constrained by a fixed set of procedures, the life of the self-employed can be full of variety. This variety of experience creates a much more human job environment, free from the uncomfortable social dynamics of an office setting.

Anyone attempting to avoid dependency on centralized authority and looking for a more independent lifestyle should consider cultivating a mindset centered on making well-thought-out investments in personal and family preparations for a life without the official life support system. At the forefront of this mindset are the so-called "preppers," who stockpile and grow food, acquire and train with weapons and invest in precious metals and other assets that can be bartered. A diverse group, preppers generally believe in living independently of the system, which they believe could collapse suddenly and without warning. While it remains to be seen to what extent their preparedness will be adequate to protect them during any of the many foreseeable catastrophic events, there is little doubt that they are already better insulated from America's unfolding bureaucratic misadventures.

The healthcare cartels

In the US, consumers already spend more on healthcare than on any other sector, including housing, transportation, food and clothing.[91] Medical expenses are a prime cause of personal bankruptcies. Numerous people are forced to hold on to jobs they hate for fear of losing access to medical care. In this climate, if we wish to remain independent, it is essential for us

---

91 http://www.bea.gov/newsreleases/national/gdp/2014/gdp3q14_3rd.ht
m

to first of all remain independent from the vampire-like US healthcare system. Let us review just how dysfunctional the bureaucratic healthcare system is in the US. Antitrust legislation, such as the Sherman Antitrust Act, the Clayton Antitrust Act and the depression-era Robinson–Patman Act were all passed to prevent price discrimination. However, over the last 30 years the health insurance industry has successfully lobbied to be granted exemptions to these laws, allowing hospitals, insurance companies and other actors in the industry to charge different prices based on a patient's ability to pay. Over time, these cartel or monopoly-like behaviors have distorted the price economy to an absolutely astounding level, to a point where it is now impossible to find out ahead of time how much any given procedure is going to cost.

Hospitals regularly charge patients with insurance a different price than those paying out of pocket. In addition, healthcare providers do not disclose prices for procedures, making sure to keep customers in the dark up until the moment they receive the bill. This prevents patients from being able to compare prices from a variety of health care providers or considering alternative treatments: since they never know the price they would be charged for a certain procedure, they have no basis for comparison. American hospitals maximize their profits by managing a complex system of floating prices for services, and by keeping it hidden.

The monopoly protections which corporate lobbyists have carved out for the medical industry have enabled them to charge outrageous prices for even the simplest procedures and products. A paper cup used to deliver pills can cost $12 each.[92] In a hospital, a single dose of Tylenol can cost $15. An EpiPen, used for treating life-threatening allergic reactions, cost less

---

92 http://ac360.blogs.cnn.com/2013/02/20/family-fights-474k-hospital-bill/

than $40 in 1986, but $400 today.[93] Meanwhile, price inflation of prescription drugs has been explosive, rising 11.8 percent in 2014 and 5 percent in 2015, putting the pinch on the most vulnerable people.[94]

State and federal finances have also seen healthcare expenditures rise exponentially. In 1980, the Federal government spent $55 billion on healthcare—not much, even after adjusting for inflation. From 1980 to 2008, the cost of healthcare rose an average of 9.1 percent a year, every year, effectively doubling every 7 years, far outpacing the country's minuscule economic growth. This exponential curve slowed only briefly after the economic crisis in 2008, but quickly resumed its outrageous climb. Today, federal spending on healthcare is over $1.1 trillion a year, nearly double the Pentagon's budget. It is expected to rise to over $1.8 trillion by 2024.

Obviously, exponential growth is unsustainable, and these healthcare expenditures will at some point become impossible, but probably not until there is a massive financial crisis and a lot of pain, both economic and physical, to go with it. In the interim, Americans are forced to acquiesce to what is possibly the largest expropriation of wealth in their history. Since healthcare is a meaningful cost to nearly every business, even the healthiest Americans are forced to bear this weight. For those of us who have to tangle with this system, the process of receiving reimbursement for healthcare expenses often turns into a nightmare plunge into a Byzantine bureaucracy, and the many medical expenses which the insurers refuse to cover is the leading cause of personal bankruptcy. According to a report published by The American Journal of Medicine in 2009, 60 percent of all US bankruptcies are the result of medical bills —and 75 percent of them went bankrupt in spite of having

93 http://billmoyers.com/2014/08/05/sticker-shock-how-big-pharma-gauges-the-american-public/
94 http://www.forbes.com/sites/matthewherper/2016/02/23/for-cvs-prescription-drug-prices-increase-less-than-expected/#264ffc362b01

medical insurance.[95]

By planning for a medical evacuation to a nation with a sane health care system in advance, you can avoid having to pay an excessive price for predictable medical care. The process isn't as difficult as it seems. The Centers for Disease Control estimates that each year roughly 750,000 US residents travel abroad for medical care, and many US hospitals partner with hospitals in other countries to help patients get the care they need.[96] According to MedicalTourism.com, which aggregates general prices for procedures around the world, prices in the US are about 10 times higher than in many South American, Asian or Middle Eastern nations.

Inside the US, there are few options for those trying to find a different path. A few hospitals like the Surgery Center of Oklahoma have a price list on their website. Their prices are far lower than other hospitals are likely to charge. Best of all, with them the patients know ahead of time how much they will have to pay. Their website states: "Transparent, direct, package pricing means the patient knows exactly what the cost of the service will be upfront. Fees for the surgeon, anesthesiologist and facility are all included in one low price. There are no hidden costs..."[97]

Remaining mobile

One of the core components of freedom is the ability to relocate whenever conditions warrant. Writer Dmitry Orlov notes that in order to be free, we need to have the ability to move about with relative ease and anonymity. "It seems uncontroversial that if you can't move, you are more or less in jail," Orlov writes. "It doesn't have to be a physical jail: you could be wearing an ankle bracelet, or just fulfill the requirement that you show up at the same place every weekday

---

95 http://www.amjmed.com/article/S0002-9343(09)00404-5/pdf
96 http://www.cdc.gov/features/medicaltourism/
97 http://surgerycenterok.com/about/

morning. Just being able to move, in a theoretical I-could-if-I-wanted-to sort of way, doesn't count as mobility."[98] Indeed, if your financial or social circumstances force you back to a location after a few days or weeks, your freedom is seriously constrained. Backed into a corner, these constraints can lead to the psychological problems we've outlined throughout this book. Therefore, to be psychologically healthy, freedom of movement needs to be more than just theoretical.

Today, American citizens are physically more stationary than ever, but at the same time our electronic devices enable us to become more and more detached from the physical world. Buzzwords like "mobile computing" and "cloud computing" don't adequately capture the pervasive nature of this separation and isolation. The wonderful new gadgets mean that hardly any of our activities still require us to be physically present in any specific location. Working in physical proximity to other people is now mostly seen as irrelevant, and the idea of meeting with other people in a traditional office setting is now seen as outmoded and inefficient. Many of us are able to do our jobs from anywhere. While theoretically this should allow us to move about as we wish, in fact, it will paradoxically make all movement suspect in the eyes of the government. If most of the citizenry can be told to "shelter in place," for reasons of national security, without impacting productivity in any way, then why not do just that? The only people that will still be allowed to move about—maintenance and delivery personnel—can already be strictly monitored using GPS tracking.

Since our mobility has essentially been limited to a few rooms, our connection to other people and to the surrounding community has suffered. Instead feeling interconnected with other people, we are interconnected with figures, diagrams, excel spreadsheets, and, of course, written rules—all of which are non-human and ultimately unconcerned with our well-be-

---

98 http://cluborlov.blogspot.com/2014/02/the-good-life-mobility-anonymity-freedom.html

ing or sanity. If you look up from your screen, wander out into the world and attempt to examine it directly, you would notice that there has been a clampdown on anonymous travel. Car license plates are scanned wherever you drive, you can no longer purchase plane tickets with cash and facial recognition technology identifies you even within crowds. There has been a general willingness among the courts to weaken protections for the average motorist against unjustified stops and searches. And once you end up on the officials' radar, you re-main there forever, and your ability to move about gradually disappears.

Compassion, understanding, kindness and other forms of positive human contact were essential for the survival of no-madic tribes. Forcibly keeping them stationary effectively undermined them. Today, Americans are not only highly station-ary, but live large portions of their lives disconnected from all of humanity—in essence, disembodied. The effect of this on the human psyche isn't difficult to guess.

Since this is what life in the US is turning into, why stay? If your personal circumstances permit, you can leave the United States for a nation where bureaucratic mismanagement of so-ciety is less pronounced, and where normal human interaction has not been disrupted by invasive, ever-watchful gadgets. Not every nation prizes administrative efficiency and technocratic control as the defining values of life. Historian and social critic Morris Berman made this point after he left the US for Mexico. Speaking in an interview with Alternet, he said:

> Here's what the US lacks, which I believe Mexico has: community, friendship, appreciation of beauty, crafts-manship as opposed to obsessive technology, and—de-spite what you read in the American newspapers—huge graciousness, a large, beating heart. I never found very much of those things in the US; certainly, I never found much heart. American cities and suburbs have to be the most soulless places in the world. In a word, America

has its priorities upside down, and after decades of living there, I was simply tired of being a stranger in a strange land.[99]

Still, perhaps the greatest motivator for people looking to leave the US isn't social but economic. In recent years, record numbers of Americans have renounced their citizenship to avoid onerous new tax reporting requirements for overseas bank accounts and possessions. An estimated 3,415 people renounced their citizenship in 2014, a 14 percent jump over the previous year.[100] According to the Federal Registrar, which issues reports on the number of Americans expatriating, 3222 have done so in the first three quarters of 2015, indicating that it will likely be another record-setting year.[101]

The easiest way to begin your transition out of the US is to acquire a work visa through your future employer. Necessary qualifications vary by country, but teaching English abroad is still one of the easiest ways for relatively non-skilled Americans to get a job abroad. The pay isn't great, but it's an easy way to get your foot in the door and determine if you really like your chosen country. Simply doing an internet search for "teach English abroad" will bring up numerous sites that specialize in providing jobs to would-be teachers.

As an example, those who are dead set on leaving the US for another developed country should consider Singapore. The nation has a reputation for minimizing bureaucratic obstructions to commerce. Once you have a job or start your own business, residency can be approved rather quickly. There is an income tax, but overseas gains are not taxed, nor are there are taxes on capital gains or interest.

---

99 http://www.alternet.org/economy/why-american-empire-was-destined-collapse
100 http://www.cbsnews.com/news/a-record-number-of-americans-are-renouncing-citizenship/
101 FederalRegistrar.gov, "Quarterly Publication of Individuals, Who Have Chosen To Expatriate, as Required by Section 6039G"

Moreover, Singapore has an atmosphere of creative energy and is especially welcoming to Americans looking to escape the imperious tax system in the US. Libertarian businessman Jayant Bhandari writes that Singapore is a great spot for Americans seeking independence from the government. "Virtually everything dealing with the government is done on the Internet in an extremely efficient and friendly way. I have never encountered a busybody from the government, and sightings of the police are rare to none."

Other benefits of Singapore include its world-class healthcare system. The World Health Organization nation ranked Singapore 6th in the world in "overall health system performance."[102] Bloomberg News ranked Singapore the most efficient healthcare system in the world in 2014. The United States ranked 44th.[103]

Other noteworthy countries include Ecuador, where the cost of living is exceptionally low, and Mexico, which features a population just short of 1 million US expatriates—more than any other nation. Of course, the easiest escape logistically and socially is probably Canada, but Canada is so tied to the US that you may find that it won't allow you to escape the increasingly global phenomenon of bureaucratic insanity.

Financial isolation

The dangers in dealing with insane bureaucracies tend to increase in times of economic distress and uncertainty.

President Obama said during his 2016 State of the Union address that "Anyone claiming that America's economy is in decline is peddling fiction."[104] You don't need to be an expert in finance to recognize that the US, and the global economy, are in trouble. As he spoke, interest rates had been set at

---

102 http://www.who.int/whr/2000/en/whr00_en.pdf
103 http://www.bloomberg.com/visual-data/best-and-worst//most-efficient-health-care-2014-countries
104 https://www.youtube.com/watch?v=PndJjTCDJmw

emergency levels—near zero percent—for about 7 years, bringing ruinous losses to pension funds, insurance companies and all individuals and institutions that require a steady yield on safe investments. And now Europe is setting interest rates below zero, penalizing savers for simply keeping their money in the bank, with the US set to follow.

Simultaneously, government insiders are pushing to further restrict the use of cash. Former Treasury Secretary Larry Summers recently suggested eliminating the $100 bill—a first step toward eliminating the use of all cash, thus destroying your ability to keep your financial transactions secret.[105]

Numerous constraints on how you conduct your financial affairs are in the pipeline. But there are still ways to preserve your wealth and to avoid the depredations of an increasingly invasive financial bureaucracy. The most obvious way is to remove some of your assets from banking institutions which can block your access to them without notice, and even confiscate them. In a worst case scenario, leaving money in the bank can result in a permanent loss of access to your savings. If you think this sounds particularly outrageous, just consider that it has already happened in Cypress where a large percentage of depositor accounts were seized to steady the country's banks. These so-called "bail-ins" use previously untouchable depositor accounts to recapitalize failing financial institutions.

The US already has a similar plan in place. In December 2012, a joint report by the FDIC and the Bank of England released a report titled, "Resolving Globally Active, Systemically Important, Financial Institutions." It argued that in the event of a collapse of a major bank "unsecured debt from the original creditors" could be transformed into "equity"—worthless stock, that is. They concluded: "New equity holders would take on the corresponding risk of being shareholders in a financial institution." In other words, funds in savings accounts could

---

105 https://www.washingtonpost.com/news/wonk/wp/2016/02/16/its-time-to-kill-the-100-bill/

be seized to help recapitalize the bank while forcing depositors to become stockholders of a failed financial institution. Ironically, they praise their plan as a valid way to avoid "the need for a bailout by taxpayers."[106] The lawful approach of letting insolvent banks fail, liquidating them and sending the bankers who violated the law to jail, as was recently done in Iceland, is not even being considered.

With so many financial parasites eating away from us, healthy economic activity gradually becomes impossible. Economist Michael Hudson argues that part of the reason for our minuscule economic growth is due to the excessive constraints on individual financial autonomy. "How on Earth can American industry be expected to compete when employees must pay 40 percent of their wages on debt leveraged housing, about 10 percent more on student loans, credit cards and other bank debt, 15 percent on FICA, and about 10 to 15 percent more on income and sales taxes? Between 75 and 80 percent of the wage payment is absorbed by the FIRE[107] sector before employees can even start buying goods and services. No wonder the economy is shrinking!"[108]

Clearly, transnational financial bureaucracies are not planning to improve your financial flexibility or to protect your interests, but are instead working hard to ensure their own continued dominance at the cost of your continued impoverishment. Decoupling from them as quickly and as thoroughly as possible is not just psychologically healthy—it is essential for your financial security. Of course, such disengagement from banking institutions and other financial officialdom carries certain risks, but the alternative—to trust these institutions to look out for your best interests when they have no motivation to do so—carries a hefty risk of total loss.

---

106 http://www.bankofengland.co.uk/publications/Documents/news/2012/nr156.pdf
107 Finance, insurance and real estate
108 http://michael-hudson.com/2012/05/paul-krugmans-economic-blinders/

People are finding ways to preserve their wealth and get their business done without paying the exorbitant, hidden American Banker Tax. The list of the tricks they use is already long and is only getting longer. There are now techniques for avoiding insolvent, predatory financial institutions: from Google Wallet, to Bitcoin, to internet banks based in Singapore, to deposit certificates issued by bullion vaults in other countries, to transacting in "junk" silver US coin.

The possession of precious metals like gold and silver are a nice hedge against the relative instability of fiat currencies and a precarious banking industry. While the paper price for these investments hasn't been spectacular in recent years, a growing global community of banking system skeptics, including many central bankers, has been finding them increasingly attractive. In a world without cash, interest-bearing deposits or privacy, it makes sense to have a store of value that is widely respected, compact and easy to transport. Even in today's debt-driven society most Americans still recognize the value of gold. In extreme circumstances, many would accept it in exchange for goods or services.

While relocation, avoidance, and other forms of physical resistance are important, none of them are really adequate to fully escape from bureaucratic insanity—unless you are willing to permanently relocate to an isolated cave. Worse, bureaucratic madness and its associated illnesses are a global phenomenon. Despite the efforts of humanists, reformers and radicals, American-style bureaucracy has been winning. So complete has been its reordering of human activity that there is little hope left for reforming our schools, corporate offices or government institutions. It would be irresponsible to pretend otherwise. But it would also be irresponsible to suggest that, just because institutional changes are highly improbable, there is nothing for us to do. If human dignity still has value, then it is worth protecting and preserving what is left of it here and now. Having meaning in life is not about developing a power base or using force to transform the establishment into something a bit less lethal. Real meaning can only come about from cultivating healthy and respectful values within us.

Deprograming your mind

If you slow down a film to a tenth or a twentieth of normal speed, you can clearly see that it is made up of a series of still images linked together to create the illusion of motion. We know that these moving visions are not real, but they provide an illusion of constructed reality which we accept. Movies are simulacra of life that we can enjoy without mistaking its images for reality. But living within a bureaucracy, which is likewise only a simulacrum of real life, based on the temporary acceptance of social machines as something real, can sometimes seem like the only possible reality—and a very unpleasant one at that!—that we can never hope to escape. This book slowed down the bureaucratic horror flick and exposed the illusion that gives rise to the bureaucratic system, perhaps giving you a chance to direct your own movie instead of being an unwilling spectator of the given one.

For most of us, total avoidance of all bureaucracy would be very difficult, perhaps impossible. Family obligations, health or financial problems, or simple anxiety about moving abroad anchors people to a physical location. But even they have many options to resist these institutions. You may be thinking, "What good is it to change my mental state if I am still stuck in a meaningless job or surrounded by an unenlightened community?" But there are many practices which can help to rehumanize us even as we struggle. Those who are willing to make major life changes to avoid the countless minor insults and the dehumanization caused by bureaucracies gone mad could benefit immensely from developing a perspective and become resigned to, if not comfortable with, the system's more unavoidable absurdities.

It isn't enough to escape the physical rules and constraints placed on us by bureaucracies. The psychological programing within each of us can be as much of a prison as the worst cubicle job or micromanaged organizational function. Even when bureaucracies are physically absent, we can unconsciously internalize their rules, undermining our sense of self-worth and warping our value systems. The challenge then is to find healthy ways to reject these meta-beliefs (beliefs about beliefs) and instill in ourselves a healthier perspective. Any method that promotes emotional honesty, self-confidence, and self-esteem will help you achieve a state of mind in which you will be able to more easily resist these warped value systems.

There are two complementary therapies designed to help you fortify your psyches against the pressures of a hyper-controlled society. I've used these to some degree and can personally testify to their effectiveness, but I would encourage you to develop your own action plan—one that is within your comfort level and draws on your strengths.

Hypnosis

Certain therapies challenge our beliefs about what is and what is not good behavior. Hypnosis is the most direct, and probably the easiest, way to quickly transform your unconscious attitudes.

While many of us consciously know that our society places on us unhealthy pressure to conform, to obey immoral rules and to seek efficiency at the cost of humanity, it is quite another thing to really know, deep down, that it is wrong—to let that knowledge percolate through us, and to begin to feel good about resisting. Our subconscious minds often tell us that we are not worthy of respect unless we do not make a certain amount of money, or pursue a certain type of career, or espouse to a widely held political belief. We doubt our ability to survive without the approval of our bosses and our families. Many of us lack the self-esteem and confidence necessary to stand up for ourselves or for others who come under attack from the bureaucratic machine. Hypnosis works by directly changing these meta-beliefs, making us more confident in whatever decisions we choose to make.

Hypnosis is a widely misunderstood practice. This is mainly due to magic shows and television portrayals which show it as a sleep-like trance. object. In fact, it is safe to assume that you spend some part of every single day in a hypnotic state at some point every day of your life. Have you ever sat and watched television for more than a few minutes, shutting out all other distractions and focusing your attention on what is happening on the screen. If the show is especially engaging, you may even feel as though you are there. From an observer's point of view, you appear to be in a trance. Watching television is not *like* hypnosis; it *is* hypnosis. It generates similar levels of brain activity as a hypnosis session aided by a professional hypnotist.

If you attempt to use hypnosis as a therapeutic tool, your attention won't be focused on the fictional worlds created in television studios, but on your own mind. Most hypnotists' patients are aware participants throughout the process. The patient is guided through a series of relaxing breathing and visualization techniques, after which positive affirmations are communicated to the person's subconscious mind which can change the patient's subconscious beliefs about themselves or the outside world.

With the help of a professional hypnotist, audio recordings, or self-hypnosis books, readers can be led to direct their focus inward, empowering them to lose harmful habits or belief systems. For example, hypnosis is often used to help people quit smoking by convincing their subconscious minds that tobacco smoke is revolting or unappealing. Others use it to lose their fear of flying or of visiting the dentist. For some people only a single session is needed to get results. You should consider hypnosis as a method to improve self-esteem, confidence, and perhaps to develop a stubborn sense of resolve—because these are essential when standing up to a dehumanizing bureaucratic system!

Hypnosis is probably the single most important device I've used to address the discrepancy between my conscious and unconscious beliefs. I always thought that society's values were wrong and that my life had value even if I refused to play by its rules. After using hypnosis to directly address these concerns, I know my own worth. I can chart my own course in life without worrying about the disapproval of others or the nagging fear of failure. Hypnosis can be effective by itself, but it can also be easily combined with other forms of therapy to maximize results.

Meditation

Our society's love of rules is rooted in our desire for security and predictability. Because American bureaucrats are looking for some kind of stable sense of meaning and purpose, they simply can't accept the fluid and ever-changing nature of life. When the complexities of life get in the way, bureaucrats react aggressively, sometimes violently. They attempt to constrain life, to lock things into place with rules. But their effort is, in the end, futile. In Buddhist thought, the only thing that is permanent is change itself, and failing to accept this reality leads to suffering. The desire to control everything that can be controlled leads to suffering for everyone involved, especially when artificial rules inevitably fail to account for every situation.

If bureaucratic insanity is unavoidable, we need to develop methods to deal with its maddening absurdities. The solution is not to develop new, more complex rules, but rather to become comfortable with lack of fixed rules, with physical insecurity and ceaseless change. Meditation can help you become aware of your compulsion to control everything, and to overcome it.

Remember, the rage expressed by many Americans comes from an unconscious self-hatred which they are often incapable of expressing. By meditating, they can develop a sense of self-awareness and eventually become at peace with themselves. Only if we are at peace with ourselves, can we then act caringly toward others. Meditation can give us a sense of perspective and enable us to be compassionate when facing difficult teachers, customers, students or bosses and to recognize and address our feelings before they become suppressed. As Buddhist teacher and doctor of clinical psychology Jack Kornfield observed rather succinctly: "Everyone has to first discover the root of anger and hatred inside themselves before they can understand how it operates in the outside world... Meditation is not a luxury or an escape from the world, but it is a deepening sense of our responsibility to learn how not to be caught by these forces."[109]

Religious practice can also serve as a counterbalance to bureaucratic insanity, but only for some. But meditation, used as a secular tool, can help to alleviate the subconscious pressure to always be in control. If they could eliminate the compulsion to lock everything down with rules, the kinds of inflexible and sadist actions we often see from teachers, police and other rule-enforcers would disappear. Of course, we can't very well make SWAT teams meditate, but we can keep ourselves flexible, de-stressed, and compassionate through regular meditation. In the long run, this will allow us to better deal with intransigent bureaucracies which for the time being aren't showing any signs of going away.

There are different types of meditation. There is awareness meditation, which allows for conscious interpretation of our own feelings. By being alone with ourselves, we can put the absurd rules of our society into context and more easily ignore them. Another favorite of mine is the lovingkindness meditation, which allows people to develop a deep well of positive

---

109 Jack Kornfield, *Meditation for Beginners*, p. 85

emotions from which they can direct onto others or draw on for themselves when dealing with difficult bureaucrats.

A book I've found useful introducing me to meditation is Jack Kornfield's *Meditation for Beginners*. Though there are surely many fine texts on meditation, Kornfield's book contains little or no filler, is under a hundred pages, and includes a CD with over an hour of guided meditations.

Art

Political critic Lionel Trilling once said that art's primary function "is to liberate the individual from the tyranny of his culture in the environmental sense and to permit him to stand beyond it in an autonomy of perception and judgment." Art gives you the space to breathe in what otherwise seems like a suffocating roboticized culture. For this reason, I rank the creation and preservation of art very highly. Art is an essential component of any plan to rehumanize society. Art startles us; it stirs up emotions; it demands that we devote our attention to something completely irrational and unproductive. In this way, the arts are counter-revolutionary. They restore value to something which, to the bureaucrat, doesn't seem to matter much: the human soul.

For a visual depiction of this process, take a look at José Clemente Orozco's mural "The Epic of American Civilization" at Dartmouth College. It depicts the circular nature of American history. From left to right, he starts with the nomadic tribes and the ancient human sacrifices of the Aztec. As the painting moves left, Orozco's painting portrays the arrival of Europeans, the establishment of Christianity, mass industrialization, and eventually, modern human sacrifice in the form of endless war. In the final panel, a man stands with axe in hand over a pile of discarded gods. His skin is peeling away from his body. It is not clear what, if anything, comes next.[110]

---

110 http://imgur.com/a/mCURI

Such art is a physical manifestation of society's dreams. It doesn't create a new reality but exposes to criticism our buried subconscious. The best art does not create idols for us to fawn over, but tears them down and subjects us to truths we would otherwise ignore. Developing an appreciation for art early on inoculates one against the materialistic belief that only the quantifiable and the material has any value. While most US states require art education as a part of the student curriculum, it has been deemphasized to satisfy testing requirements instituted by the No Child Left Behind Act of 2001. In the period immediately following the law's passage, participation in music courses fell 46 percent in California and the number of music teachers declined by 26.7 percent, even though school enrollment had increased.[111]

At the heart of any plan to restore vitality and decency to ourselves must be the restoration of truth—not necessarily the kind of truth that is imparted through good news reporting or the reading of scholarly books, but the kind of truth that comes from knowing ourselves and from reenergizing the part of ourselves that can feel pain. Art gives us the strength to feel and know that pain. Art is sometimes the only kind of heroism that remains open to us when we face a tyranny this all-encompassing. Only once we become aware of our own poverty of the soul and learn to express it can we bear witness to the broader poverty of the soul that is blighting our world.

Pablo Picasso once said that painting is an act of war, by which he did not mean an assault on humanity but rather an act of rebellion in defense of it. "Painting is not done to decorate apartments," he said. Instead, the artist works to bear witness to "the heartbreaking, passionate or delightful things that happen in the world, shaping himself completely in their image." Unlike the artist, the materialistic-minded thinker cannot value or think in such abstractions. The very act of being

---

111 http://www.edutopia.org/arts-music-curriculum-child-development

an artist is a direct assault on the valueless entities of a mechanized society.

If we attempt to instill an early appreciation for the arts, we can provide young people with the power to resist a soulless mindset. Through the arts, we are empowered to explore our psyches without any false pretense to making ourselves useful or to being productive. Art's ethereal qualities allow it to be a humanizing agent in our society.

"When we revolt it's not for a particular culture. We revolt simply because, for many reasons, we can no longer breathe."
—Frantz Fanon

12. Community

America today can be said to in a state of what Camus called "metaphysical rebellion"—a rejection of reality as it is lived. Many of us have a deep-seated sense that we are justified in rebelling against all the numerous restrictions on how we live. We want to live our lives without having all of our options dictated to us. But outward rebellion is forbidden to us, driving it inward, in a cycle that breeds depression, addiction, alienation and violence.

As a release valve for this building internal pressure, a number of counterculture experiments have been gaining in prominence, placing an emphasis on person-to-person interactions. The intent of these experiments is to reignite a passion for life and to lift the persistent numbness and boredom that have become so common in our society. Despite intermittent disapproval from society's more puritanical elements, experiments with what anthropologist Victor Turner called "anti-structure" have continued to gain prominence.

Forms of rebellious anti-structure include living a relatively nomadic lifestyle. Though this can be extremely isolating, it purifies all remaining interactions by eliminating the need to maintain appearances and cultivate relationships just for show. Not content to disengage and wander the interior of a decadent society, many people leave the United States for another part of the world, joining the ranks of the millions of American expats. Less permanent experiments with anti-structure include Thoreau-style off-grid living and large-scale camping events.

A modern example of this phenomenon can be observed in the annual Burning Man event: every year, for a little over a week in late summer, thousands of people create a temporary community in the uninhabited desert of Nevada, some 100 miles north of Reno. There they camp out in a drug-fueled carnival of countercultural excess. They selflessly gift resources to each other, and, true to the name, they burn a massive effigy of a human figure, burning "the man" both literally and figuratively. Participants are urged to "leave no trace," emphasizing harmony with each other and with nature.

Burning Man now gathers over 60,000 people every year, up from only a few hundred in the early 1990s. Smaller-scale "burns" have sprouted up around the country as well, usually occupying campgrounds with several hundred people for a four-day weekend. The intent isn't just to have a fun weekend excursion, but to cultivate an alternative identity and to catch a glimpse of a new way of life.

Mark Peterson, an anthropologist at Miami University, described these experiments as being focused on creating a new identity:

> One loses one's old identity, formed by normative social categories such as class, race and gender; and freely and spontaneously encounters others. After such an experience, the person ultimately returns to the place from which he or she had come (reaggregation), often in a socially transformed way.[112]

---

112 Mark Peterson, "In Search of Antistructure",
https://www.academia.edu/5460315/In_Search_of_Antistructure

Burning Man is a kind of symbolic, estheticized rebellion in which, instead of expressing their rage and indulging in violence, participants emphasize a sense of fellowship and communal solidarity. Many of the participants feel oppressed by society's controlling elements—a unification born in chains. "When he rebels," Camus wrote, "a man identifies himself with other men and so surpasses himself." This is the real human nature in action: to build communities based not on conformity, but on respect for individuality and autonomy.

Critics have charged that Burning Man has grown too fast, abandoning its message in favor of cultivating a party atmosphere and, in the process, increasing the number of rules and regulations participants must follow. Competing cliques of artists and partiers create tension in a community which many say is no longer civil. But overall, Burning Man and its sister events can still be consid-

Albert Speer
testifying at Nuremberg

ered a healthy reaction to a society utterly obsessed with conformity and control, especially when paralleled against the alternative methods for restoring identity, which can involve violence or fanaticism. Of course, it's impossible to know if any of this helps people practically resist the pressures that inevitably return when we return to work or school, but Burning Man points us in a good direction: toward developing an alternative system of values and at least occasionally escaping the mundane, rule focused life.

"The rebels of our day are criticizing the very foundations of society which have hitherto been held sacred, and first and foremost amongst them that fetish, law."
—Peter Kropotkin

Afterword: Regaining your dignity

What hope does any one person have in standing up against a system that is so big—and growing bigger every day? It is easy to slip into a nihilistic depression. None of us wants to relinquish our individuality, to grow up into a world where carefully constructed scripts determine the course our careers and choose for us who we must hate and who we are allowed to love. Yet here we are, awash in rules, laws, and pressures to conform so numerous that they threaten our very sanity. Fortunately, once we are aware of them, we can make the conscious choice to live and love without regard for these dictates.

If you are curious enough to be reading about bureaucracy and its effects on society, you are already well positioned to question and reject these dominant ideas. You can say no to military service in support of pointless, endless wars, or refuse to take part in exploitative or dishonest practices at your place of work. You can choose to be patient with children and others who have not yet learned how to navigate labyrinths of inane rules. You can train yourself to see bureaucratic systems for what they are and then work to carefully repudiate their claims on your soul, if not your body. At the very least, you can avoid agitating or crossing the path of zealous rule enforcers who don't have your level of insight and compassion. These may seem like small, imperfect victories, but they may be enough to infuse your life with meaning.

If you find yourself inside an insane bureaucracy, getting out is an obvious objective, but it is not the only one. You can choose to stay and fight—to be a teacher that actually reaches students or police officer who protects the rights of the public. This path is not easy, but by resisting bureaucratic machines— by adhering to our own sense of morality—we can be still seek liberation as individuals. If we are lucky, we can even help to free people we care about from this dehumanizing system. In these ways, we imbue our lives with meaning. Better yet, by actively resisting, we can inspire others to choose the more difficult path which is so often the right one.

For those unable or unwilling to change course, the only remaining options are denial and despair. It seems that most people prefer denial. When someone complains about their job, how often have you heard these excuses: "I have no choice"; "I need the money"; or the ever-popular "I have no right to complain because others have it so much worse than I do!" These are all powerful arguments, because on some level there is clearly some truth to them. But they are also a form of self-hypnosis. Change may be tough, but not impossible. But it becomes downright impossible once you tell yourself that it is impossible.

At a commencement address at Georgetown University, writer and TV show producer David Simon noted: "To commit to a just cause with no hope of success is absurd. But then... not committing to a just cause is equally absurd. But only one choice offers the possibility for dignity. And dignity matters. Dignity matters." It can be enormously dispiriting and de-pressing for an honest, autonomous human being to be forced b y circumstances to function within a soul-destroying social machine, but surrender to it leads to a rage-filled, self-hating madness.

Defending your dignity is not without cost. Being in touch with your emotions at a time when society is destroying everything that is vulnerable, ethereal and non-commodified means living with sadness. In times of great emotional tribulations, it is the stoic personality that stands the best chance of surviving —for a while anyway—but you cannot have true dignity without being in touch with your feelings. "Despair is the only cure for illusion," Philip Slater wrote. "Without despair we cannot transfer our allegiance to reality—it is a kind of mourning period for our fantasies. Some people do not survive this despair, but no major change within a person can occur without it." If you decide to feel, to be generous in spirit, to find ways to circumvent or ignore the rules and to learn chart your own path, you will find yourself empowered and your life infused with new meaning. More than anything, our rejection of our venomous bureaucratic culture pushes us learn to feel and to love again.

58274693R00110

Made in the USA
Lexington, KY
06 December 2016